The Supported Learning in Physics Project
has received major support from

Ford

Esso

IEE

ESSEX

Nuclear
Electric

The project is also supported by
The Department for Education and
Employment

SUPPORTED
LEARNING
IN PHYSICS
PROJECT

The Open
University

D1390351

PHYSICS
IN
SPACE

This unit was written by
Bob Kibble and Steve Miller

YORK
SIXTH FORM
COLLEGE

Heinemann

THE SUPPORTED LEARNING IN PHYSICS PROJECT

Management Group

Elizabeth Whitelegg, Project Director, The Open University

Professor Dick West, National Power Professor of Science Education, The Open University

Christopher Edwards, Project Coordinator

Professor Mike Westbrook, Vice-President for Education, Industry and Public Affairs, The Institute of Physics

George Davies, Manager, College Recruitment, Ford of Britain

Geoff Abraham, Project Trailing Manager

Dorrie Giles, Schools Liaison Manager, Institution of Electrical Engineers

Martin Tims, Manager, Education Programme, Esso UK

Catherine Wilson, Education Manager (Schools and Colleges), Institute of Physics

Production

This unit was written for the Project by Bob Kibble, Coulsdon College, Old Coulsdon, Surrey, and Steve Miller, University College London.

Other members of the production team for this unit were:

Elizabeth Whitelegg, Project Director and Academic Editor

Christopher Edwards, Project Coordinator

Andrew Coleman, Editor

John Coleman, Course Assessor

Alison George, Illustrator

Maureen Maybank, Unit Assessor

Julie Lynch, Project Secretary

Sian Lewis, Designer

Cartoons supplied by ABC Cartoons

ISBN 0 435 68843 X

The Institute of Physics, 76 Portland Place, London, W1N 4AA.

First published 1997 by Heinemann Educational Publishers.

Printed in Spain.

For further information on the Supported Learning in Physics Project contact the Information and Marketing Officer, The Centre for Science Education, The Open University, Walton Hall, Milton Keynes, MK7 6AA.
1.1

CONTENTS

The SLIPP units introduce you to a new method of studying – one that you may not have used before. They will provide you with a way of studying on your own, or sometimes in small groups with other students in your class. Your teacher will be available to guide you in your use of this unit – giving you advice and help when they are needed and monitoring your progress – but mainly you will learn about this topic through your own study of this unit and the practical work associated with it.

We expect that you will study the unit during your normal physics lessons and also at other times – during free periods and homework sessions. Your teacher will give you guidance on how much time you need to spend on it. Your study will involve you in a variety of activities – you won't find yourself just reading the text, you will have to do some practical work (which we have called 'Explorations') and answer questions in the text as you go along. (Advice on how long each exploration is likely to take is given.) It is very important that you do answer the questions as you go along, rather than leaving them until you reach the end of a section (or indeed the end of the unit!), as they are there to help you to check whether you have understood the preceding text. If you find that you can't answer a question, then you should go over the relevant bit of text again. Some questions are followed immediately by their answers but you should resist the temptation to read the answer before you have thought about the question. If you find this difficult it may be a good idea to cover up the answer with a piece of paper while you think about the question. Other slightly longer or more demanding questions have their answers at the back of the section. You are likely to need help with these; this might be from a teacher or from working with other students.

It will be up to you to make notes on the physics you have learnt from this unit as you go along. You will need to use these notes to help you revise. You should also keep notes on how you arrived at your answers to the questions in the unit. It is important to show all your working out for each question and to set it out clearly, including the units at every stage. We try to do this in our answers to the questions in this unit.

Most sections start with a short 'Ready to Study' test. You should do this before reading any further to check that you have all the necessary knowledge to start the section. The answers for this test are also at the end of the section. If you have any difficulties with these questions, you should look back through your old GCSE notes to see if they can help you or discuss your difficulties with your teacher, who may decide to go over certain areas with you before you start the section or recommend a textbook that will help you.

The large number of practical explorations in the unit are designed to let you thoroughly immerse yourself in the topic and involve yourself in some real science. It is only after hands-on experiences that you really begin to think about and understand a situation. We suggest that you do some of these explorations with other students who are studying the unit and, when appropriate, present your results to the rest of the class. There are a large number of these explorations and it may not be possible for you to do all of them, so if everyone shares their results with others in the class you will all find out about some of the explorations that you are unable to do.

Your teacher will arrange times when the practical work can be undertaken. For health and safety reasons you must be properly supervised during laboratory and kitchen sessions and your teacher will be responsible for running these sessions in accordance with your school's or college's normal health and safety procedures.

HEALTH AND SAFETY NOTE

The unit warns you about any potential hazards and suggests precautions whenever risk assessments are required of an employer under the Management of Health and Safety at Work Regulations 1992. We expect that employers will accept these precautions as forming the basis for risk assessments and as equivalent to those they normally advocate for school science. If teachers or technicians have any doubts, they should consult their employers.

However, in providing these warnings and suggestions, we make the assumption that practical work is conducted in a properly equipped and maintained laboratory and that field work takes account of any LEA or school or college guidelines on safe conduct. We also assume that care is taken with normal laboratory and kitchen operations, such as heating and handling heavy objects, and that good laboratory practice is observed at all times.

Any mains-operated equipment should be properly maintained and the output from signal generators, amplifiers, etc., should not exceed 25 V rms.

Space is big – big enough to include a lot of physics. This unit will help you to understand some of the basic principles of advanced physics and appreciate how they relate to worlds beyond Earth. Each of the following four sections will focus on a particular set of ideas. Section 2 explores atoms and in particular the nuclear physics at the very heart of an atom. Energy from the nucleus is the source of the power that drives stellar evolution and dictates the life and death cycles of stars. You will also learn how a supernova can teach us about radioactive decay processes. Quantum physics permeates Section 3. In this section you will discover how astrophysics uses the messages in the spectral lines produced by stars to formulate models of cosmic evolution. Newton's law of universal gravitation dominates Section 4, applying to everything in space from the Hubble Space Telescope to comet Shoemaker–Levy 9. Finally, Section 5 acknowledges that all our theories about space rest on information received through the electromagnetic spectrum, in particular using visible wavelengths and optical telescopes.

Here is a summary of the physics you will cover in this unit:

- radioactivity
- nuclear fusion and fission
- absorption and emission spectra
- quantum effects
- the electromagnetic spectrum
- the photoelectric effect
- wave–particle duality
- Newton's laws of motion
- universal gravitation
- force, field and potential
- satellites
- refraction of light
- diffraction by apertures
- resolution using optical instruments
- the passage of light through optical systems.

Also, throughout the unit we have incorporated the theme of the public awareness of physics in space, as outlined in Section 1.1 overleaf.

Astronomy is, quite literally, astronomical; it is big science and it deals with big questions. At its largest, it deals with the Universe, and so it claims to deal with universals. According to the current most popular theory, the Universe began several billions of years ago with a Big Bang – an enormously energetic fireball in which the Universe, space and time were created. Since that time it has been expanding, though whether it will expand for ever or, one day, start to collapse back on to itself in a Big Crunch, no one yet knows. And there are many gaps in our scientific knowledge about the stages between the Big Bang and the present day.

Remember that space is just one of the many arenas in which physics operates. We have used space here as our context, but be aware that physics goes beyond space. The physics you learn here will apply in every corner of your home, in every college and university and in every industrial research laboratory. It is perhaps this fact that enables physics to unite all the branches of science. As a physicist you will have something to say about the very tiniest subatomic particle and the most remote quasar. Yes, space is big, but physics is even bigger.

1.1 Space, science and the public

Over the past ten years or so there has been increasing concern about the lack of understanding of science among members of the public. There have been worries that Britain is falling behind its international competitors because not enough young people are choosing scientific subjects at school and the country's workforce is failing to pick up the skills needed to design and manufacture high-technology goods. Scientists themselves fear that a public unappreciative of science is becoming less and less willing to fund expensive scientific research projects out of their taxes. How, in a democratic society, can people who are not aware of the nature or facts of science make sensible decisions about issues such as the safety of the nuclear industry or the right way to use genetic engineering? Cultural historians point to a growing gap between the 'scientifically literate' and those who are largely ignorant of – or even hostile to – science. This gap, they say, may prove dangerously divisive. For these, and many other reasons, organizations such as the Royal Society – Britain's premier scientific society – have launched programmes to increase public awareness and appreciation of science.

One area of the physical sciences that still – even, increasingly – manages to capture the public imagination is space. And so, in this unit, we have included some questions and exercises on the public understanding of science. Since the media are essential in bridging the gap between research science and scientists and the public, some of these exercises take the form of investigating the way newspapers have covered various issues of general interest. We have also given you interviews with some of the scientists who made the news themselves, so that you can get some idea of what they feel about their work and the way it has been portrayed in the media. In tackling these questions and exercises, you should be aware that there are not necessarily right answers in the strictly mathematical sense. Instead, the questions are designed to allow you to explore some of the wider issues around science in general, and space and astronomy in particular. There is a role for good communicators of science in the media and the public can learn a lot of science from accurate and interesting reporting.

The study of space is physics on the largest scale imaginable. But in this section you will start your exploration of space at the opposite extreme, with a look at the nature of matter at the scale of the atom and nucleus, and base your understanding on discoveries made in Earthly laboratories. Why start small? First, if we are to make any sense of cosmological events we have to agree about the laws that govern them and decide if our scientific laws are universal; that is, true for galaxies as well as in our laboratories. So far the answer seems to be yes – no inconsistencies crop up if we assume that the same laws are obeyed everywhere. So your findings about Earthly matter will apply to the matter found in stars and galaxies.

What are the driving forces that power a star? What happens when a supernova explodes? These are two of the questions addressed by this section. The centre of a star is a hot place, perhaps 15 million degrees. At this temperature atoms of hydrogen move fast enough to fuse together when they collide to form helium atoms. This is the start of a process that has produced every element known to science. The energy released by nuclear fusion powers every star and galaxy in the Universe, yet on Earth we have yet to imitate fusion in a useful controlled way. However, nuclear fission has been achieved, and in this unit you will learn how these two processes are related to forces within the nucleus of an atom. Radioactive elements are by-products of both nuclear fission on Earth and of supernova explosions in space. In this section you will trace the story of supernova 1987A to learn about the physics of radioactivity.

NUCLEAR PHYSICS IN SPACE

READY TO STUDY TEST

Before you begin this section you should be able to:

- discuss the structure of matter in terms of atoms and molecules
- describe an atom in terms of nucleus, protons, neutrons and electrons
- calculate the weight of a mass
- calculate the change in gravitational potential energy of a mass near Earth's surface using mgh
- use $E_K = \frac{1}{2}mv^2$ to calculate the kinetic energy of a moving mass
- describe the nature and properties of alpha, beta and gamma radiations and represent them in equations using standard notation such as in the equation overleaf showing the emission of a beta particle $\left(\beta^+ \text{ or } \begin{pmatrix} 0 \\ 1 \end{pmatrix} e \right)$ and a neutrino (v) from the combination of two hydrogen molecules:

$$^{1}_{1}\text{H} + {}^{1}_{1}\text{H} \rightarrow {}^{2}_{1}\text{D} + {}^{0}_{0}v + {}^{0}_{1}\text{e}^{+}$$

- explain what the atomic number and mass number (or nucleon number) of an isotope are
- explain the difference between stars, galaxies and planets.

QUESTIONS

R1 (a) Draw a sketch to show how arrangements of atoms can help to explain why crystals have smooth geometrical shapes.

(b) Describe why the smell from a gas leak will spread even without draughts or convection.

R2 Explain in what way it might be said that 'atoms are mainly empty space'.

R3 Figure 2.1 shows a dog, mass 20 kg, at the foot of some stairs.

(a) Copy Figure 2.1 and draw arrows showing the forces acting on the dog while it is stationary at the foot of the stairs.

Figure 2.1
What forces are acting on the dog?

3.0 m

(b) Explain why the dog is described as being 'in a state of equilibrium'.

(c) Calculate the weight of the dog. (Use $g = 9.81 \text{ N kg}^{-1}$.)

(d) Calculate the change in gravitational potential energy when the dog moves from the bottom to the top of the stairs.

R4 If you were designing a protective glove to protect a worker from radiation given out by a radioactive mineral, what material would you choose if the mineral were known to emit the following (explain your choice): (a) only alpha radiation, (b) beta and gamma radiation?

R5 If an alpha particle and a beta particle were to be travelling at the same speed which would have the greater kinetic energy? Why?

R6 Explain the significance of all the letters and numbers in this equation:

$$\text{Th} \rightarrow {}^{234}_{91}\text{Pa} + {}^{0}_{-1}\text{e}$$

R7 You will have heard of stars, galaxies and planets. Look at the following list and sort out which objects belong to each category (you may need to use a reference book or a CD-ROM to help find out about some of these objects): Earth, the Milky Way, Jupiter, Proxima Centauri, the Sun, Betelgeuse, Pluto, M100.

2.1 Ideas about atoms

The idea of a smallest indivisible particle was taught by a Greek scientist and thinker called Democritus about 2000 years ago. He decided that if the world was made of matter that was infinitely small it would be impossible to cut an apple, and so he introduced the idea of an **atom** as the smallest indivisible particle. Since those early days scientists have made good use of the idea of atoms to explain all sorts of phenomena, from why crystals exist to why air has pressure and, of course, most of chemistry. As a result, the basic idea of atoms has evolved. Figure 2.2 shows some of the interpretations of an atom that have supported physicists' theories.

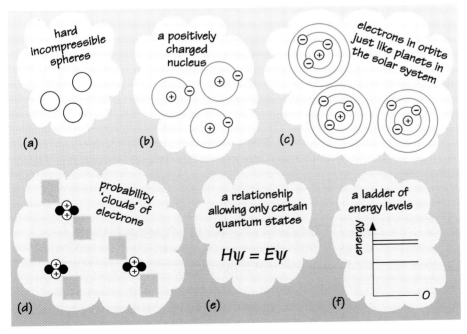

Figure 2.2
Interpretations of an atom

11

As the problems facing science have become more complex, so the scientists' **model** of an atom has changed. The model starts as a 3D 'picture' to help us visualize what it might look like, but it eventually needs to be considered as a graph or even an equation. So where does this leave us? What exactly is an atom?

 Which of the models in Figure 2.2 is correct?

The answer to this puzzle is that they are all correct. Being a good physicist means being able to be flexible in your choice of model. Choose the one that best explains what you need to explain. None is wrong, all are right – in their own way. The key is to know the limitations of your model. (In fact (a) to (f) shows a sequence of how we represent the atom, with each model in the sequence becoming more complex as our understanding develops.)

Q1 Figure 2.3 shows a model of the No. 73a bus route.

(a) What is the real strength of this model? What does it do well?

(b) Give two features of the 73a bus route that are not provided by the model. ◆

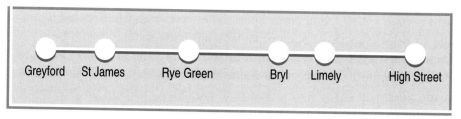

Figure 2.3
No. 73a bus route

Q2 You are probably familiar with the atomic explanation for gas pressure. It is based on the idea that particles move randomly, hitting the walls of the container as they move.

(a) Which of the models for atoms in Figure 2.2 is most appropriate for this explanation?

(b) If you use the solar system model shown in Figure 2.2(c), can you imagine what might happen as one atom collides with another? ◆

Q3 'Science is about facts. A scientist will tell you the right answer because it is his or her job to find out the truth. I didn't want to study physics because it is all about facts that we already know about' (17-year-old sixth-form student). Is there any truth in this view? Discuss this with a friend. ◆

2.2 What holds an atom together?

However we decide to model the inside of an atom, it is agreed that particles known as protons, neutrons and electrons can be found there. It is also agreed that it is difficult to split atoms. Yet **supernova** explosions occur that involve huge forces and temperatures; matter is broken apart and new elements created. To understand what might be going on we have to consider the forces that hold particles together in the first place. There are two basic forces available to us: gravitational and electrical.

On such a small scale, with particles of mass of the order of 10^{-27} kg, although the familiar force of gravity between particles is indeed present, it is far too small to be considered. The positive and negative charges on protons and electrons will cause an **electric force** of attraction between them. The law governing these forces was found by Charles Augustine de Coulomb in 1777 – you can read about his work in the SLIPP unit *Physics Phones Home*.

Coulomb's law is an example of an 'inverse square law'. Figure 2.4 illustrates a typical calculation using Coulomb's law. Notice the $1/r^2$ term. This means that when the separation of two charges doubles, the force between them decreases four times (it is quartered).

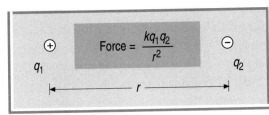

Figure 2.4   Coulomb's law

Q4 (a) Use Coulomb's law to calculate the size of the electrical force between an electron and a proton. (An atomic radius is about 1.0×10^{-10} m and the magnitude of both proton and electron charge is 1.6×10^{-19} C. The constant $k = 9.0 \times 10^9$ N m^2 C^{-2}. If you have a scientific calculator, you may find some of the constants that you will need in this unit already in its memory.)

(b) The gravitational attraction between electron and proton is about 10^{-48} N. How can this be said to be 'far too small to be considered'? ◆

Q5 If gravity is such a weak force, how can it be responsible for holding the Universe together? ◆

Q6 Earth is full of atoms that each have balanced positive and negative charges. Why do we not need to consider these electrical forces when calculating the forces between bodies in space such as the Sun and the Moon? ◆ ○

The **nucleus** of an atom poses an even greater challenge to physicists. At first glance, it looks as if the positive charges on protons should cause them to repel each other. As you have seen, we can't use gravitational forces to hold the particles together. The nucleus ought to fall apart, but it doesn't.

It was not until well into the twentieth century that a short-range force was proposed. A force that acts over distances the size of the nucleus, about 10^{-14} m. This force, known now as the **strong nuclear force**, is believed to act between all **nucleons**. (A nucleon is the term we use for either protons or neutrons.) The strong nuclear force is thought to be one of the three fundamental forces in nature.

Q7 The strong nuclear force must be at least strong enough to overcome the repulsion between two protons in the nucleus. Use Coulomb's law to make an estimation of the magnitude of the strong nuclear force between two protons separated by a nuclear diameter, about 1.0×10^{-14} m. ◆

2.3 Nuclear energy

You probably already know something about nuclear power and power stations. This section looks at the origin of this energy source – the nucleons themselves.

Nucleons (neutrons and protons) can exist as separate, free particles or bound together in the nucleus of an atom in very much the same way that a piece of rock can exist wandering freely through space or as an ornament in a domestic garden rockery.

What interests physicists is the question 'is there any energy advantage in nucleons being "bound" or being "free"?' It appears that there does exist a most stable arrangement for nucleons – to be in a group of about 56. This nucleus with about 23 protons and 33 neutrons is found in an atom of iron. So, an iron atom of iron-56 contains the most stable nucleus, see Figure 2.5. (**Atomic number** is the number of protons in the nucleus.)

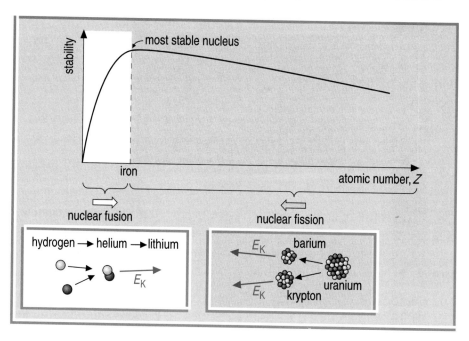

Figure 2.5
Graph of stable nuclei against atomic number

Given enough energy to separate and rearrange themselves, all nuclei would eventually reform to produce nuclei of iron. This means that nuclei heavier than iron, say a nucleus of uranium, will tend to break up to become smaller while nuclei less massive than iron, say hydrogen, will tend to join others to become more massive. It is this tendency to reach a more stable configuration that is the basis of both the **nuclear fission** and the **nuclear fusion** processes.

In both cases, nuclear fission and nuclear fusion, there is a transformation of mass into kinetic energy. This is where the energy comes from to generate electricity in a nuclear power station (nuclear fission) and how energy is transformed to power the Sun and all other stars (nuclear fusion). In each process the mass of the nucleons falls slightly. (A free nucleon has a greater mass than one bound to others in the nucleus of an atom.) The missing mass, called the **mass defect**, appears as kinetic energy of the reaction products. Einstein's famous equation shows how the amount of energy E, can be calculated from a mass defect, m.

$$E = mc^2$$

where c is the speed of light in a vacuum, 3.0×10^8 m s^{-1}.

Q8 During a typical fusion process the mass of a nucleon might fall by 1.26×10^{-29} kg. Calculate the release of energy when four nucleons fuse to form a helium nucleus. ◆

Q9 There are approximately 10^{26} nucleons in the water in a cup of tea. If they were each to undergo the mass defect given in Question 8, would this release enough energy (about 70 000 J) to boil this water to make the cup of tea? ◆

Q10 Margie's Cafe in Belmont market serves 80 cups of tea each working day. Could the energy from fusion of nuclei in a single cup of tea provide Margie with enough energy to run her business? For how long? ◆

 The calculations above ought to reveal the potential of energy from nuclear fusion. However, it seems to contradict the law of conservation of energy. How can energy be created where none existed before?

Before Einstein proposed the equation $E = mc^2$ in about 1915, this would indeed have been an issue. But physicists are now comfortable with the idea of energy and mass being two manifestations of the *same* entity. In our macroscopic world of cars, books, food and drink the distinction is more easily made, but in the microscopic world of nuclei there is yet another opportunity for a flexible approach to the two words. You must be able to juggle to be a good physicist – juggle with ideas.

2.4 The Sun – a lesson in nuclear fusion

Nuclear fusion is the process that powers the Sun and all stars. A star can typically spend about 10 thousand million years as a Sun-like star undergoing nuclear fusion before going supernova. It is by far the most common nuclear reaction in the Universe, and this can be appreciated when one realizes that 99% of the mass in the Universe is in fact hydrogen and helium.

It is in the centre, the core, of a star like the Sun that the temperature is high enough, about 15 million K (the K represents **kelvin**), for nuclear fusion to take place. The many stages in the fusion process are complex, but a simplified scheme might be:

$$\text{Stage 1} \quad {}_{1}^{1}\text{H} + {}_{1}^{1}\text{H} \rightarrow {}_{1}^{2}\text{D} + {}_{0}^{0}v + {}_{1}^{0}\text{e}^{+}$$

The symbol H represents an atom of hydrogen, which contains a single proton (the atomic number is given by the subscript '1') and has one massive particle in its nucleus, i.e. the proton. The **mass number** (or **nucleon number**) is shown as the superscript '1'. D is deuterium, an **isotope** of hydrogen known as 'heavy hydrogen'. Its nucleus contains a proton and an additional neutron. A **neutrino** 'v', and a **positron** 'e^{+}' are also produced in this process. The positron e^{+} will soon meet an electron and the two will annihilate, giving off a gamma-ray (γ). The neutrino will travel out of the Sun and into deep space.

$$\text{Stage 2} \quad {}_{1}^{1}\text{H} + {}_{1}^{2}\text{D} \rightarrow {}_{2}^{3}\text{He} + \gamma$$

At this stage a new element, helium (He), is produced, but not in its most stable form.

$$\text{Stage 3} \quad {}_{2}^{3}\text{He} + {}_{2}^{3}\text{He} \rightarrow {}_{2}^{4}\text{He} + 2{}_{1}^{1}\text{H}$$

Here a more stable isotope of helium is produced from the reaction of other lighter helium isotopes.

At each stage there is a mass defect as the nucleons combine. The process started above would continue, making heavier and heavier elements such as beryllium, lithium and eventually iron.

At each stage the mass of the products is less than the mass of the original nuclei. The result of the mass defect is the energy released as photons in the Sun's radiation. These photons will be absorbed, re-emitted and scattered as they travel from the Sun's core and it may take a photon 20 million years to emerge from the outer surface. Much of the Sun's radiation is in the infrared part of the electromagnetic spectrum. This is why sunlight seems so 'warm' to us. Hotter stars than the Sun tend to be brighter, but their energy is detected as mainly shorter wavelengths, such as visible and ultraviolet. Section 3 'Quantum physics in space' discusses this in more detail.

The Sun is constantly losing mass. The present rate of mass loss is about 5.0×10^9 kg s^{-1}.

Q11 Use Einstein's equation to calculate the power output of the Sun. ◆

Q12 The mass of the Sun is currently estimated at 2.0×10^{30} kg. Is there any danger that the Sun's mass will run out in our lifetime? Calculate how long it will take to use up all the mass if the fusion process continues at the same rate. ◆

Meanwhile, the Sun, and indeed all other stars, will continue in a state of dynamic equilibrium between two opposing pressures. The **radiation pressure** forcing the gas outwards being balanced by the attractive forces of gravity, as shown in Figure 2.6. This equilibrium phase in the life of a star will last about 10 000 million years. A star going through this phase is known as a **main sequence** star.

Eventually the radiation pressure in the Sun will be reduced as the hydrogen in the core runs out. It will then collapse under its own gravity and the core will heat up rapidly causing it to explode into a **red giant**, engulfing the inner solar system and 'roasting' Earth. Estimates indicate that the Sun is unlikely to do this for a further 5000 million years – fortunately.

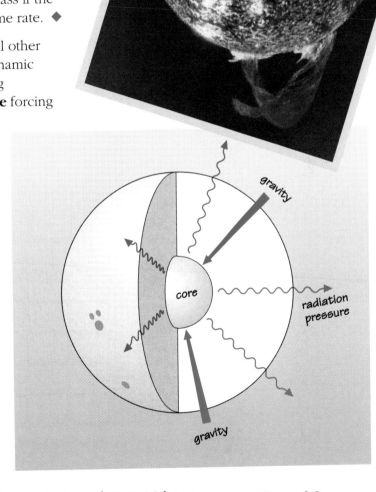

A solar flare

Figure 2.6
Equilibrium state of a star

 The surface temperature of the Sun is about 6000 K. Make an estimate of the temperature of a red giant star.

A reasonable guesstimate would be less than 6000 K. Radiation in the red end of the spectrum is emitted by cooler objects (just think of the colour changes when heating up a piece of wire in a Bunsen flame). A sensible value might be 3000–4000 K.

During the final phases from red giant to the obscurity of a cool rocky mass, the star will undergo further nuclear fusion, producing carbon, neon, oxygen, silicon and eventually iron. For some red giants the final collapse will produce a shock wave resulting in an explosive burst: a supernova. The star might emit energy at the rate of a small galaxy for a short period of a few days. Such outbursts are rare occurrences for Earth-bound observers, but there are recordings of such events, the most recent being Supernova 1987A, which you will learn more about in Section 2.9.

2.5 Nuclear fission – a source of power nearer home

In Figure 2.5 we showed that heavier nuclei will be naturally unstable and will tend to produce lighter nuclei as they decay to a more stable iron nucleus. This was first achieved in a controlled experiment by Enrico Fermi and his team working with uranium at the University of Chicago, in December 1942 (see Figure 2.7). Today there exists an entire industry built on the instability of the nucleus of uranium-235. About 17% of the electricity you use today will have been produced from a nuclear reactor.

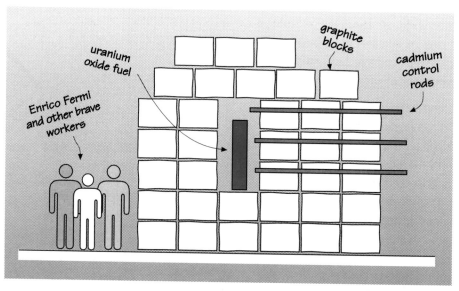

Figure 2.7 Enrico Fermi's experiment. The uranium fuel heated up by its own internal nuclear fission. The cadmium rods absorbed neutrons and so could slow down the process as they were pushed further into the graphite 'pile'. The graphite blocks protected Fermi and his team from stray particles such as neutrons

In a fission reactor the uranium fuel rods contain artificially enriched uranium-235, the fuel having been processed from uranium ore. The fuel rods are housed in the reactor core and the process of fission is triggered by firing a neutron into the core. Figure 2.8 shows this process.

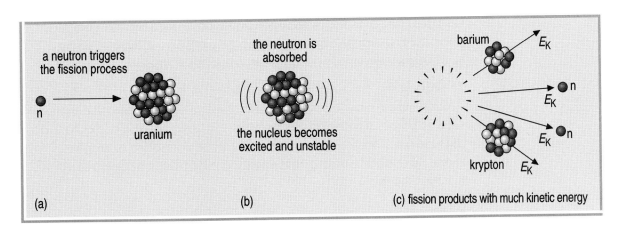

(a)

(b)

(c) fission products with much kinetic energy

This process is described by the equation

$$^{0}_{1}n + ^{235}_{92}U \rightarrow ^{144}_{56}Ba + ^{90}_{36}Kr + 2\,^{1}_{0}n$$

The kinetic energy of the **fission products** holds the key to nuclear power. The mass defect when nucleons are rearranged into smaller nuclei results in the products of fission moving with much greater velocity. It is this kinetic energy of fission products that heats up the reactor core. The energy is transferred by a cooling fluid, which can be water, liquid sodium or carbon dioxide, depending on the type of reactor.

To keep this process continuing it is important that each fission impact releases additional neutrons to maintain the fission process and so ensure a chain reaction, as shown in Figure 2.9.

Figure 2.8
The nuclear fission process

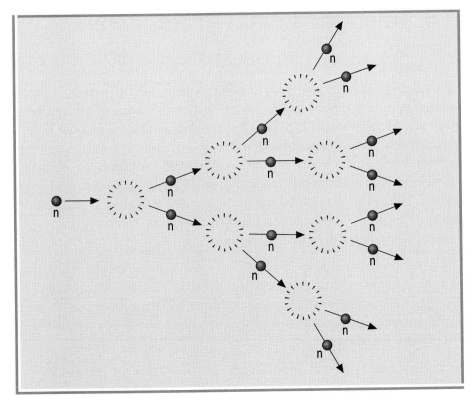

Figure 2.9
A chain reaction

If such a chain reaction were to be left uncontrolled the uranium might overheat catastrophically, resulting in an explosive release of energy. This is, of course, designed to happen in a nuclear warhead.

To prevent the uncontrolled chain reaction in a nuclear reactor the neutrons are controlled by a number of control rods made of a material such as boron, which absorbs neutrons. By lowering the boron control rods into the core, the fission process can be controlled or stopped. This is one method of ensuring that energy output from a nuclear reactor matches the demand.

 Give some reasons why a country's demand for energy might fluctuate during a day.

The morning breakfast routine demands energy to boil kettles and make toast. The evening routine again boils millions of kettles, cooks million of meals and switches on millions of TVs.

The mass of a nucleon in a nucleus of ^{235}U is greater than the mass of the same nucleon when in a nucleus of, say, krypton, a fission product. The mass defect is responsible for the release of energy during fission.

Q13 If the mass defect is about 1.0×10^{-30} kg per nucleus, estimate: (a) the energy possible from the fission of a single ^{235}U nucleus, (b) the energy possible from the fission of 1.0 kg of ^{235}U. (0.235 kg of ^{235}U contains about 6.02×10^{23} nuclei.) ◆

2.6 Unstable nuclei – radioactive decay

As you read this page your body is being bombarded by particles. Of course, most of these are molecules in the air you are breathing, but you must add to these many dozens of fast-moving particles that result from the naturally occurring **radioactive decay** processes in your surroundings. This is known as the **background radiation**. In addition, there are neutrinos from the Sun and cosmic rays from the centre of the galaxy. You are even contributing to the general background radiation yourself because a small proportion of the atoms in your body are radioactive. You are giving off radiations.

There are three main types of radiation resulting from natural radioactive decay. They are called alpha, beta and gamma radiations and you are likely to have learned something about them and their properties in your GCSE courses. Question 14 invites you to brainstorm all you know about these three radiations.

Q14 Make a copy of Table 2.1. Beneath each heading make brief notes from your own knowledge of radioactivity. Compare your notes with those of another student. Fill in any gaps in your knowledge. ◆

Type of radiation	Exactly what is it?	What are its particular properties?

Table 2.1
Sample table for Question 14

The word 'radiation' can cause confusion. Light from a candle or from the Sun 'radiates'. This simply means that it spreads out in all directions. In understanding radioactivity the word 'radiation' has a particular meaning. It refers to the spreading out of fast-moving, alpha, beta and gamma radiations, which can ionize atoms in their path. We call them ionizing radiations. Alpha and beta radiations are traditionally associated with being a stream of particles, whereas gamma radiation is considered to be a 'ray'. The properties of alpha, beta and gamma radiation are summarized in Figure 2.10. The distinction between 'particles' and 'rays', known as 'wave–particle' duality, is explored further in Section 3 'Quantum physics in space'. Take care when using the term radiation; think carefully about what you mean.

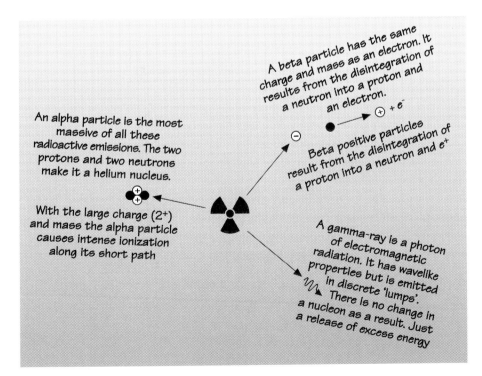

Figure 2.10
Properties of alpha, beta and gamma radiation

21

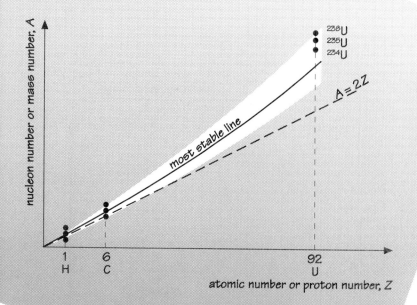

Figure 2.11
The most stable
arrangement for a
nucleus

Exactly why and when a nucleus will choose to emit a particle is impossible to say. One clue, however, is to look at the balance of neutrons and protons in the nucleus. A nucleus with many more protons than neutrons is likely to be unstable. Equally, a nucleus with far fewer protons than neutrons is also likely to be unstable. The most stable arrangement for any nucleus is shown in Figure 2.11.

You will see in Figure 2.11 that atoms with a number of different nuclei can exist for any particular element – these are called isotopes.

 (a) How many isotopes are shown in Figure 2.11 for carbon (atomic number 6)? (b) Give numbers of electrons, protons and neutrons in each isotope in (a).

(a) Three isotopes are shown: ^{12}C, ^{13}C and ^{14}C. (b) There are six protons and electrons in each isotope and 6, 7 and 8 neutrons, respectively.

In any sample of CO_2, 99% of the molecules will have carbon in the form of ^{12}C, the rest will be ^{13}C. Why are other isotopes not represented?

They each have unstable nuclei and so disintegrate to become other elements with more stable nuclei. The fact that they are unstable means that they exist in very low proportions.

We have already seen hydrogen existing as ^{1}H and ^{2}H (deuterium) (see Section 2.4 on nuclear fusion). A third isotope, ^{3}H, is tritium. A closer look at Figure 2.11 reveals some of the changes that will occur spontaneously when nuclei are unstable, see Figure 2.12.

By emitting a particle, alpha or beta, or gamma-ray, a nucleus moves to a more stable state. For light nuclei, such as ^{14}C, the move towards stability requires only a single emission.

$$^{14}_{6}C \rightarrow \, ^{14}_{7}N + \, ^{0}_{-1}e$$

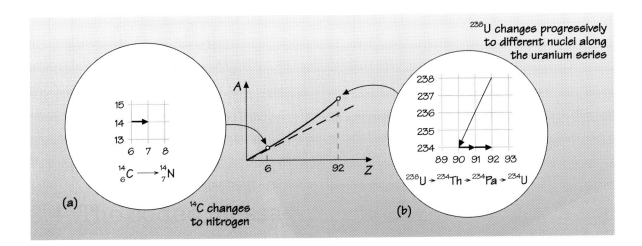

(a) $^{14}_{6}C \longrightarrow {}^{14}_{7}N$

^{14}C changes to nitrogen

^{238}U changes progressively to different nuclei along the uranium series

$^{238}U \rightarrow {}^{234}Th \rightarrow {}^{234}Pa \rightarrow {}^{234}U$

(b)

 Is this alpha or beta emission?

_____

This is beta emission; $^{0}_{-1}e$ is the notation for a particle with

negligible mass and negative charge.

Q15 Look at the first decay of uranium-238 as shown in Figure 2.12.

(a) Is this alpha, beta or gamma emission?

(b) What happens next? ◆

For a heavy nucleus, such as ^{238}U, the first emission is followed some time later by a whole series of emissions as a single nucleus proceeds to change to a new element and then to another on the way to stability, which in this case is found when it becomes a nucleus of lead, as shown in Figure 2.13. The process when a nucleus changes its atomic number by radioactive emission is called **transmutation**. New elements are formed in the decay process. During a long **decay series** the changing nucleus will also transmute to different isotopes of the same element and Figure 2.13 shows several examples of this. It is worth noting that the alchemists' dream in the seventeenth and eighteenth centuries was to turn lead ('base metal') into gold. Such a chemical transmutation was never achieved but such serious pursuits occupied the minds of great scientists including Newton.

Figure 2.12
Transmutation during radioactive decay

ALCHEMY

Alchemists spent their time trying to turn base metals such as lead or copper into silver or gold. The notion that such transformation might be possible was based on a philosophy that, under the proper astrological conditions, it was possible to 'perfect' or 'heal' lead by turning it into gold, and that by 'killing' the metal it could then be revived in a finer form. As atomic theories of matter began to be taken more seriously by physicists and chemists, alchemy was discounted and the chemical facts gathered by the earlier alchemists were reinterpreted to contribute to the basis of modern chemistry. It was not until the nineteenth century, however, that the possibility of transforming lead into gold was conclusively contradicted by science.

$$^{238}_{92}U \xrightarrow{\alpha} {}^{234}_{90}Th \xrightarrow{\beta^-} {}^{234}_{91}Pa \xrightarrow{\beta^-} {}^{234}_{92}U \xrightarrow{\beta^-} {}^{230}_{90}Th \xrightarrow{\alpha\ \alpha\ \alpha\ \alpha\ \beta^-\ \beta^-\ \alpha\ \beta^-\ \beta^-\ \alpha} {}^{206}_{82}Pb$$

Figure 2.13 Transmutations along the decay series for $^{238}_{92}U$

So, a 10 g sample of ^{238}U left on the shelf of a laboratory will contain atoms of ^{234}Th, ^{234}Pa, ^{234}U, ^{230}Th, etc., all at one stage or another in the long journey towards ^{206}Pb. Each nucleus disintegrates in a random manner, making it impossible to predict exactly when a single decay will occur. However, as a 10 g sample contains many millions and millions of nuclei, each at a particular stage in the decay series, there will be a spread of different elements at any one time in the sample.

Q16 ^{235}U is also radioactive. Its nucleus decays by alpha emission. The process can be described by the equation below:

$$^{235}_{92}U \rightarrow ? + ^{4}_{2}He$$

Say as much as you can about the nucleus that results from this decay and draw a diagram similar to those in the circles in Figure 2.12 for this decay process. ◆

2.7 The chance of a decay

It is impossible to know when a particular nucleus in an atom of ^{238}U will change into a nucleus of ^{234}Th and emit an alpha particle. In the fullness of time, of course, every nucleus of ^{238}U will have changed and changed again, eventually to become a nucleus of lead, ^{206}Pb, at the end of the decay series. However, when dealing with such large numbers we can predict the trend. We can, for example, determine how long it takes for half the original ^{238}U nuclei to change to ^{234}Th. This time is called the **half-life** of the isotope. For ^{238}U the half-life is 4.5×10^9 years. For ^{14}C the half-life is 5730 years. For ^{234}Pa the half-life is only about 72 s.

Figure 2.14 shows how the number of ^{234}Pa nuclei in a freshly isolated 10 g sample of ^{234}Pa changes with time. The shape of the curve is **exponential**. It has a property that during each equal time interval the

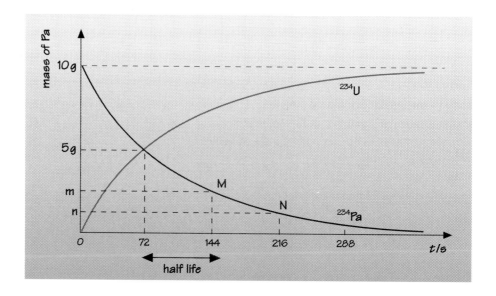

Figure 2.14
An exponential decay curve for protactinium-234

quantity changes by a fixed ratio. (Exponential curves are also called 'constant ratio' curves.) In our example after *any* interval of 72 s the number of nuclei will have reduced by a factor of 2; in this case the constant 72 s ratio being 1/2. A more rigorous explanation of exponential curves is available in Appendix 2.1 at the end of this section.

Q17 Use the definition of half-life to predict the mass of Pa at points M and N on Figure 2.14. ◆

Although Figure 2.14 shows a decrease in the number of ^{234}Pa nuclei, this does not mean that the 10 g sample is fading away from sight. The daughter product of the decay is ^{234}U, and for every nucleus of ^{234}Pa that disintegrates a nucleus of ^{234}U is produced. The total number of nuclei in the sample remains constant. They just start off as ^{234}Pa and end up as ^{234}U. The coloured curve in Figure 2.14 shows the growth of ^{234}U.

45
MINUTES

E Exploration 2.1 Investigating radioactivity

Part (i) Measuring the half-life of protactinium-234

Apparatus:

◆ sealed source containing uranium salt in solution and an organic solution ◆ Geiger–Müller tube and counter ◆ stopclock

In work with radioactive sources and materials, follow local rules for users of ionizing radiations; see local authority guidance, DfEE and Welsh Office AM 1/92, the Scottish and Northern Irish equivalents or the CLEAPSS Laboratory Handbook, Section 12.10.1. Impervious gloves should be worn while measuring the half-life of protactinium and investigating a gas mantle.

A parent nucleus of uranium-238 will decay through a long series of transmutations with one stage being the production of protactinium-234. ^{234}Pa emits beta particles and these can be detected by a Geiger–Müller (GM) tube and counter. Your sample of uranium-238 will be in a sealed polythene bottle containing the parent uranium salt solution and an organic solvent. The organic solvent will rest above the uranium salt solution. It is less dense. Shake the bottle well for 10 s and allow the two layers to separate. Place the GM tube outside the bottle next to the top (organic) layer. Start the counter and record the reading at 10 s intervals for 2 minutes.

(*Note:* Always determine the mean background count in your location before taking other measurements. Subtract the background count from any other measurements.)

The organic solvent has dissolved any of the protactinium salt that had built up in the uranium solution. When the two layers separate after shaking, the protactinium will be carried to the upper layer. The GM tube will count the natural decay of this protactinium from the upper layer. Eventually more protactinium will have been formed in the uranium salt layer and you can repeat the measurements after another shake.

Plot activity against time for 2 minutes, taking care to remove any background count from your measured readings. The time for the protactinium activity to halve can be found from your graph. This is the half-life of protactinium-234

Part (ii) Designing a paper thickness measurer

Apparatus:

◆ sealed beta source ◆ GM tube and counter ◆ 20 sheets of paper (scrap paper will do)

Place the beta source about 10 cm from the GM tube. Measure the count rate without inserting any paper. Now explore how the count rate changes as sheets of paper are added between source and detector. Record and plot your results.

Now take an unknown number of sheets of paper and place them between source and detector. Use the reduced reading to help you to make an estimate of the number of sheets you used. How sensitive is this technique? Can you distinguish between 11 and 12 sheets for example?

Part (iii) Investigating a Camping Gaz mantle

Apparatus:

◆ GM tube ◆ Camping Gaz mantle ◆ variety of lead and aluminium absorbers

The material used in the manufacture of white silk Camping Gaz mantles is radioactive. Use the GM tube and any absorbers to investigate the types of radiations given off by the mantle.

Q18 A 50 g sample of ^{234}Pa is freshly prepared and isolated. What mass of ^{234}Pa is likely to be left after 144 s? ◆

In Exploration 2.1 you used a GM tube to detect the presence of beta particles. Although individual events can be detected, it is more usual to record the rate of disintegrations averaged over a time period. This quantity is called the **activity** of the sample. Activity is measured in **becquerels**, Bq. One becquerel is a rate of one disintegration per second.

A particularly active sample might typically be measured in megabecquerels, MBq. The background count as measured using a GM tube in a typical school or college laboratory might be 0.5 Bq. It is good practice to calculate the mean background count from a number of measurements and then subtract this from subsequent results.

If an active sample has a decay product that is not going to decay, then the progress of activity over time is predictable. Only two isotopes are involved.

The activity of this sample will eventually decrease as more nuclei become stable. In a sample with stable decay products the activity will decrease exponentially. At first, when there are many nuclei available to decay many will. During this time the activity is high. After two half-lives, when about a quarter of the nuclei are yet to decay, the activity will be a quarter of its initial value.

Q19 The results in Table 2.2 show the activity of a sample of freshly isolated thoron gas recorded at 10 s intervals using a GM tube and a counter reading counts per minute. The mean background count as measured by the same GM tube that day in the laboratory was 25 counts per minute (cpm).

(a) Plot a graph to show how the activity of the thoron gas changed with time.

(b) From your graph, estimate the half-life of thoron gas. ◆

Table 2.2 Radioactive decay of thoron gas

Time/s	10	20	30	40	50	60	70	80	90	100	110	120
Decay rate/cpm	346	297	265	234	208	185	165	133	122	114	104	98

Q20 The half-life of carbon-14 is 5700 years. If the ^{14}C activity of a 10 g fresh living twig were expected to be 80 Bq, then after 5700 years this would be expected to fall to about 40 Bq. Plot the reduction in activity against time for four half-lives (about 23 000 years) and use your graph to make an estimate of the age of a twig, mass 10 g, which was found within an ancient burial tomb. The measured ^{14}C activity was 18 Bq. ◆

2.8 Supernovae and radioactive decay

Exploding stars (supernovae) are a rare occurrence. However, there are descriptions of supernovae in historical records. The supernova of 1006 was seen and recorded by astronomers across the world as was the supernova in 1054 and in 1181. On each occasion the unexpected bright star must have caused a mixture of excitement and fear.

The scholar Ali ibn Ridwan wrote in Cairo concerning the 1006 event:

> The spectacle appeared in the zodiacal sign of Scorpio, in opposition to the Sun … It was a large circular body 2.5 to 3 times as large as Venus. The sky was shining because of its light.
>
> (Marschall, 1994, p. 57)

However, in France, Alpertus of Mertz recorded:

> A comet was seen in the southern part of the sky with a horrible appearance, emitting flames this way and that. In the following year a most terrible famine and mortality took place over the whole Earth.
>
> (Marschall, 1994, p. 58)

The next significant supernova event is known as 'Tycho's star' of 1572. Tycho Brahe was a Danish astronomer and nobleman. For him the fact that there had occurred an unpredicted event meant that the very foundations of Aristotle's Greek astronomy had to be doubted. He wrote in 1590:

> I no longer approve of the reality of those spheres the existence of which I had previously admitted, relying on the authority of the ancients rather than driven by the truth of the matter itself. At present I am certain that there are no solid spheres in heaven, no matter if these are believed to make the stars revolve or to be carried about by them.

(Marschall, 1994, p. 81)

In February 1987 a giant star exploded in the southern hemisphere sky. It was the subject of much interest. The brightness of the star rose significantly as observers saw it brighten to shine as bright as stars visible with the naked eye. The intensity then fell but it was noticed that it dimmed with a characteristic exponential shape (see Figure 2.15).

Figure 2.15
The brightness of Supernova 1987A

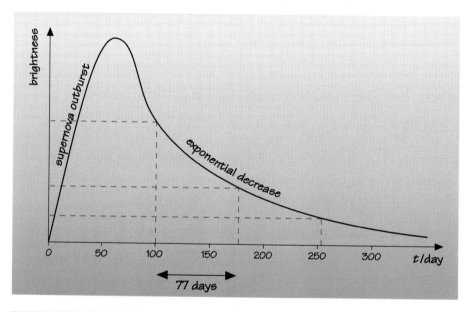

Supernova 1987A before (right) and after (left) exploding

2.9 Public science – supernovae

This giant star became known to astronomers as Supernova 1987A (SN1987A). It exploded in one of the smaller galaxies in the cluster called the Large Magellanic Cloud, to which our own Milky Way belongs. The explosion was 'only' 150 000 light years away from us, making this one of the closest supernova explosions – as these events are termed – ever witnessed since recorded history began.

By several strokes of luck, astronomical observations began within a few hours of the explosion commencing. And several other experiments picked up an intense burst of neutrinos – will-o'-the-wisp particles that interact very weakly with other forms of matter – coming from the dying star.

From the moment the astronomical community was alerted to this violent and catastrophic event, telescopes around the world were swung towards it. Measurements were taken in all available wavelengths, some – such as those using ultraviolet light and X-rays – from satellites orbiting above Earth. Astronomers were keen to see if the models that they had devised to explain how supernovae work really did correspond to what was happening in the southern skies.

Read the article 'Supernova cooks the elements' from *The Times* of 2 June 1987 (reproduced overleaf) and then answer the following questions.

Q21 What is the 'gap' identified by journalist Robert Matthews, and how do supernovae fill it? ◆

Q22 What evidence have the scientists now found to support the early astronomers' theories about heavier elements and supernova explosions? ◆

Dr Peter Meikle of Imperial College, London, is one of the world's leading experts on supernovae. During the course of 1987 he led a team of astronomers using the Anglo-Australian Telescope making infrared measurements of SN1987A as the expanding fireball crashed its way through the surrounding space. In the interview on pages 31–2, Dr Meikle explains the significance of this event to our understanding of the Universe.

Peter Meikle

Supernova cooks the elements

By Robert Matthews

Observations of the spectacular supernova explosion discovered earlier this year have given British astronomers powerful evidence in support of one of the most important theories in astronomy.

The theory aims to explain the origin of the chemical elements. All the raw components, such as electrons and protons, that make up the universe were created in the Big Bang explosion about 16 thousand million years ago, but the *combinations* of these particles, in other words the chemical elements, did not form until much later.

A few minutes after the initial explosion some of the lighter elements such as hydrogen, helium and lithium were created in the primordial oven. But conditions soon became too cool and quiescent for the other natural elements up to uranium, the heaviest, to form.

Astrophysicists therefore had to look for a hotter place in the universe that could provide the conditions suitable for such "nucleosynthesis".

They found just such an oven in supernovas. These are stars which, having used up all their nuclear fuel and started to collapse, undergo new, extremely violent reactions that blow the stars to pieces.

In 1957 astrophysicists Fred Hoyle, Geoffrey and Margaret Burbidge and William Fowler published calculations that showed that these explosions could account for the creation of the chemical elements, including those such as carbon that are vital to the existence of life.

Although the theory appears to fill the enormous gap between what the Big Bang itself could provide, and what elements were known to exist, there has been little evidence to back up the idea.

Now a team at Leicester University has confirmed the basic idea that supernovas can produce heavy elements in considerable quantity, by careful observation of the supernova discovered in February in the skies of the southern hemisphere.

By a great stoke of luck, just a few days before the explosion, a Japanese satellite carrying X-ray detection equipment built by the university and the Rutherford & Appleton laboratory near Oxford was put into orbit.

This equipment is the most sensitive yet put into orbit, and is capable of detecting relatively low concentrations of heavy elements.

Professor Ken Pounds, of the university, told *The Times* that analysis of data from the satellite has revealed the presence of the heavy element iron in the vicinity of the supernova in quantities far higher than those found in our own sun.

This is exactly what would be expected if supernovas were the sources of iron in the universe, which then becomes diluted by the force of the explosion down to the levels found in the sun.

Professor Pounds said that the latest results were "easily the strongest backing yet" for this astrophysical theory which, unlike much else in the field, has particular relevance to life on Earth.

(*The Times*, 2 June 1987)

Interview with Dr Peter Meikle

Before dealing with SN1987A itself, just what is the fascination of supernovae for astronomers such as yourself?

My primary reason for looking at supernovae is that you get extremes of conditions – of densities, temperatures and energies – that you just don't get anywhere else in the Universe. Most stars that we look at through our telescopes and attempt to model are stable. But we also need to understand why some stars explode. When you look at the stars you are seeing various snapshots of what we call stellar evolution – the way stars change with age. Supernovae give us a very extreme test of our understanding of stellar evolution.

Secondly, when we look at stars we are looking really only at the surface. But what is happening there is being driven by nuclear processes going on deep inside, and we would like to be able to 'open up' a star and see what is happening there. Supernovae do this for us – lots of the material being produced by nuclear synthesis at the centre of the star is shot out into space.

Thirdly, we think that these types of explosions are very important for distributing the elements heavier than hydrogen and helium throughout space, elements vital for life, like carbon, nitrogen and oxygen. These elements are produced in the centres of almost all stars, but supernovae, because of their extreme conditions, also produce much heavier elements such as iron, lead, uranium and gold. There is literally a little bit of a supernova inside all of us.

Fourthly, because supernovae are so bright – at their peak they may be 100 million times as bright as our Sun – we can see them from a long way away. We can see supernovae in far off galaxies, at genuinely cosmological distances. So supernovae are one of the best ways of studying the way the Universe is expanding, how fast other galaxies are streaming away from us.

What was the particular significance of Supernova 1987A? What did it tell astronomers that they did not already know?

Well, we were incredibly lucky with this supernova for several reasons. Firstly, an astronomer called Rob McNaught was actually looking at the Large Magellanic Cloud when the explosion happened. So he took a measurement of it when it was only three hours after the final explosion and the fireball was actually brightening. This was a very important measurement for our understanding of the process of supernova explosions.

Secondly, a number of detectors around the world picked up a burst of neutrino radiation and were able to measure the spread of energies they had. This proved that the explosion really was caused by what we call a core collapse – we had this as a possible mechanism for supernovae since it was first put forward by Fred Hoyle in the 1940s. But this was the first direct evidence that core collapse really was the right model.

Thirdly, SN1987A is the only case where we know exactly which star it is that has exploded. Received wisdom was that red supergiants would go supernova; in fact the star which exploded to form SN1987A was blue and not nearly as luminous as we thought would have been necessary for such a large explosion. Nor did it have as massive a cloud of hydrogen gas as we would have predicted.

By following what happened to SN1987A we have been able to clear up a lot of the uncertainties about supernovae. For a start, we did not know what kept them so bright for so long. If you take a fireball expanding at 10 000 kilometres per second, it should cool after two days to such an extent that you would not be able to see it. But supernovae stay hot and bright for several months.

What was causing this to happen, we thought, was the radioactive decay of nickel, first into cobalt, and then into iron. During the months that followed SN1987A we were able to follow this process using gamma- and X-ray astronomy, and our own infrared measurements at the Anglo-Australian telescope. The results agreed perfectly with the mechanism for making cobalt and then iron from nickel.

You've talked about the mechanism of the supernova explosion being due to 'core collapse'. Can you explain what you mean by this?

OK, let's talk you through the final days of a star that's going supernova. About two days before the explosion, the star's centre has a complicated layered structure. Going in from the outside, you have a layer where hydrogen is being burnt to form helium. Then you get a layer where this helium is being turned into carbon and oxygen. These elements, in turn, are being burnt to neon, which itself gets converted to silicon. And finally, silicon is being processed to form iron, which is the heaviest element that you can form by nuclear synthesis, while still releasing energy.

At this point, the star is 100000 times brighter than the Sun, but, in addition to this, vast amounts of energy are being given off as neutrinos. In fact 10 million times more energy is coming out as neutrinos than is given out as visible light.

Now, there comes a point at which the iron core right at the centre of the star reaches a mass of 1.4 times that of the Sun. This point is called the Chandrasekhar Limit, named after the famous Indian astronomer. Although the core is more massive than the Sun, it is so dense that it occupies only the volume of Earth. The temperature is 1×10^{10} K and the density is 1×10^7 kg m^{-3}. But the force due to gravity is now so great that the electrostatic repulsion due to the electrons orbiting the iron nucleus is not able to resist it.

The core goes into 'free fall'. In just 10 ms, the core collapses from being the size of Earth to being just the size of London. The density, at 5.0×10^{11} kg m^{-3}, is that of an atomic nucleus. The temperature is now 6×10^{10} K. The collapsing core 'bounces' off itself, sending a shockwave throughout the entire star. This, coupled with the vast numbers of neutrinos being formed as electrons and protons are crushed together to form neutrons, causes the final 'core collapse' explosion.

Given the enormous violence of a supernova, what sort of danger would we be in should one go off in our own galaxy?

Well, you can calculate that we ought to get a supernova in our own galaxy about once every 200 years. But since the last one we observed was the Crab supernova about 1000 years ago, you could say we are overdue one. That would be very exciting, but – in that sense – would not be a surprise.

As to danger, if we had a supernova explode as close to us as the Sun – if the Sun went supernova – you would never see. The neutrino burst would kill you first. If one went off just 10 light years away, you would have to worry about the radiation flash. The main problem would be that the ultraviolet flash would strip away Earth's protective ozone layer, and then we would all be fried. The estimated recovery time from that is about 100 years, and what would then be around to take over the world is anyone's guess.

That said, I am still a supernova enthusiast. I look on the work I did on SN1987A as some of my best. It is a reminder that physics in the Large Magellanic Cloud is the same as the physics in our world. It is a great testimony to the universality of the laws of physics.

Q23 You are a reporter on a broadsheet newspaper (such as the *Guardian* or *Telegraph*) who has carried out the above interview with Peter Meikle. Pretend this is February 1987, and you are the first with the news. Using some of his words as direct quotes and paraphrasing the rest, explain the mechanism and significance of supernova 1987A in an article of just 300 words.

(*Remember:* You need to give your readers a sense of the scale of the event by reference to everyday objects and events. For instance, at $10\,000$ km s^{-1} you could fly round the world in four seconds.) ◆

You can find more information on supernovae on NASA's pages on the Internet. See the Further Reading and Resources section at the end of the unit for web addresses.

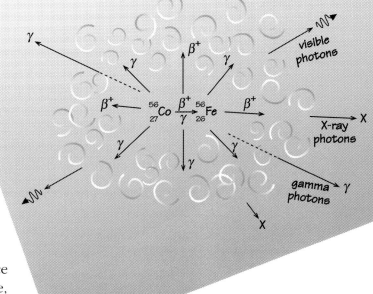

Figure 2.16
The radioactive decay of cobalt-56

Could radioactivity play a part in supernova outbursts? (*Note:* The intensity of SN1987A fell exponentially and the half-life of the measured supernova intensity was about 77 days.)

The observed intensity of SN1987A precisely matched the expected decay of the isotope cobalt-56, which has a half-life of 77 days. Could it be that heavy isotopes such as cobalt-56 are produced in supernova explosions? It appears so. The model emerging from the study of SN1987A is of an unstable star in the last stages of life exploding and forming a large quantity of nickel-56 as well as emitting visible radiation enabling us to detect the explosion. This decays naturally to cobalt-56 and then to stable iron-56, producing enough gamma radiation to heat up the surrounding gas, making it glow and emit more visible and X-ray photons. Figure 2.16 shows the radioactive decay of cobalt-56.

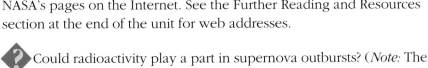

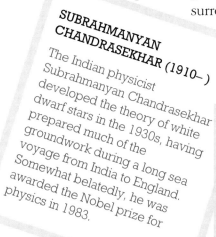

SUBRAHMANYAN CHANDRASEKHAR (1910–)

The Indian physicist Subrahmanyan Chandrasekhar developed the theory of white dwarf stars in the 1930s, having prepared much of the groundwork during a long sea voyage from India to England. Somewhat belatedly, he was awarded the Nobel prize for physics in 1983.

If this model is correct, then some time after the initial outburst we ought to detect a stream of X-rays and gamma radiation coming from the supernova as the disintegration of nickel and cobalt gets under way. Following the visible evidence, both the Soviet space station MIR and the Japanese X-ray satellite GINGA confirmed the X-ray outburst coming from SN1987A. The gamma-rays were detected by the solar maximum mission satellite launched in 1980. The evidence seems conclusive for a model of supernovas as producers of heavy isotopes whose decay is responsible for the **light curve** now characteristic of a supernova star.

Q24 Consider two helium nuclei separated by 2.0×10^{-9} m as shown in Figure 2.17.

(a) Use Coulomb's law to calculate the size of the electric force acting between them. Is this force attractive or repulsive?

(b) If the two nuclei were to move to 2.0×10^{-8} m apart, what would happen to the magnitude of the electric force between them?

(c) We express the mass of nuclear particles using an atomic mass unit, u, which is equal to 1.66×10^{-27} kg. A single neutron has a mass of 1.00866 u and a single proton has a mass of 1.00728 u. The total mass of the four separate nucleons in an alpha particle is 4.03188 u and the mass of the complete helium nucleus is 4.001504 u.

Use this data to show that the work required to separate an alpha particle into its individual nucleons is almost 30 MeV. (1 eV = 1.6×10^{-19} J.) This is also the value for the binding energy of an alpha particle. ◆

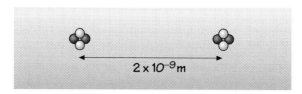

2×10^{-9} m

Figure 2.17 Helium nuclei

Q25 In a typical fission reactor neutrons interact with fissile uranium-235 and with non-fissile uranium-238.

(a) What is the distinction between 'fissile' and 'non-fissile'?

(b) Explain the significance of the numbers 235 and 238.

One product of this interaction might be a nucleus of Neptunium, produced by the reaction shown below:

$$^{238}_{92}\text{U} + ^{1}_{0}\text{n} \rightarrow \text{Np} + ^{0}_{-1}\text{e}$$

(c) Explain how the nucleus of neptunium would be different from the nucleus of ^{235}U.

(d) The nucleus of neptunium will itself decay into a nucleus of plutonium by the emission of a negative beta particle. (i) What is the mass number of the resulting plutonium nucleus? (ii) What is the atomic number

(e) Explain the role played by control rods in a controlled fission reactor. ◆

Q26 Figure 2.18 shows the brightness of an imaginary supernova, SN1991B.

(a) Describe in words the variation in brightness from day 2 to day 5.

(b) Explain why it could be thought that the power supply behind the bright star might be the decay of a radioisotope. Give evidence to support your answer.

(c) If SN1991B was 18 million light years from Earth, when did the star first explode?

(d) SN1991B also emitted gamma-rays. (i) Explain what a gamma-ray is. (ii) What type of change in a nucleus would accompany the emission of gamma-rays?

(e) The number of recorded sightings of supernova stars has increased dramatically over the last 30 years. More have been discovered during this short time than in the previous thousand years. Explain what this fact has to say about: (i) the changing Universe, (ii) astronomy on Earth. ◆

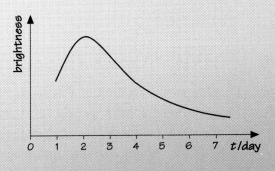

Figure 2.18
Brightness of supernova 1991B

Q27 There is evidence of much confusion among the general public on the subject of radioactivity. You have the task to offer simple but correct explanations to the public on the following issues. For each issue make a clear explanatory statement to explain the confusion.

(a) 'I read that the smoke alarm in my new home uses alpha radiation. I know that radiation from the Sun is harmful, especially the radiation that causes skin cancer.'

(b) 'I am worried about having an X-ray. The operator wears a lead apron and hides behind a concrete wall when the X-ray photo is taken. I don't get any protection at all. Am I at risk?'

(c) 'There is a nuclear power station just along the coast from where we go for our summer holiday. I am worried about the nuclear bombs stored inside.'

(d) 'My daughter Shirley came home from school today and explained that the teacher had been showing the class a radioactive source. Is there any danger that Shirley will become radioactive herself?' ◆

Achievements

After working through this section you should be able to:

- discuss the value and limitations of atomic models with confidence
- describe the processes of nuclear fission and nuclear fusion, naming the main elements usually involved in each process
- perform calculations concerning mass defect, electric forces and half-life
- relate the nuclear fission and fusion processes to energy production in a power station and the Sun, respectively
- understand the changes that occur in the nucleus of a radioisotope
- appreciate some of the dangers and properties of radioactive isotopes
- interpret exponential decay curves in terms of changes to nuclei
- relate Earthly nuclear physics to situations in space
- appreciate how some scientific events are represented by the media.

Glossary

Activity The rate of disintegration of a radioisotope.

Atom Thought by the Greeks to be the smallest indivisible particle. The twentieth century has uncovered many more 'elementary' particles smaller than an atom.

Atomic number The number of protons in a nucleus.

Background radiation The radiation naturally existing in our environment from building materials, rocks, cosmic rays, etc.

Becquerel, Bq A measure of activity equal to one disintegration per second.

Coulomb's law A relationship to enable the magnitude of the electric force to be calculated. The relationship is expressed by the formula $F = \dfrac{1}{4\pi\varepsilon_0}\dfrac{q_1 q_2}{r^2}$ or, more simply, $F = \dfrac{k q_1 q_2}{r^2}$, where the constant $k = 9.0 \times 10^9$ N m^2 C^{-2}, q_1 and q_2 are the two charges and r is the distance between them.

Decay series The repeated emission of particles from a nucleus causing it to transmute many times towards a stable element.

Electric force The attraction or repulsion of charged particles.

Exponential A pattern of change that has a constant ratio property.

Fission products The results of splitting an atom of uranium into smaller particles.

Half-life The time it takes for the number of active nuclei to reduce to half the original value. This is also the time for the activity to reduce by half.

Isotope Nuclei with different mass numbers due to the presence or absence of some neutrons.

Kelvin The unit of temperature on the Kelvin scale, which uses the same intervals of temperature as the Celsius scale, but has its zero at absolute zero.

Light curve The variation in brightness of a star – particularly a star such as a supernova, which varies considerably.

Main sequence A star in the middle of its life when the main fuelling process is hydrogen fusion.

Mass defect The reduction in the mass of nucleons in a fission or fusion processes. The mass appears as kinetic energy.

Mass number The number of nucleons (neutrons and protons) in a nucleus. Also known as nucleon number.

Model   Used throughout science to help us to picture or simplify an idea.

Neutrino   A subatomic particle with zero mass and charge.

Nuclear fission   The break up of a nucleus into smaller nuclei after being excited by a collision with a neutron.

Nuclear fusion   The process of joining together nuclei to form nuclei of heavier elements.

Nucleon   A proton or a neutron.

Nucleon number   The number of nucleons (protons and neutrons) in a nucleus. Also known as mass number.

Nucleus   The central core of an atom containing the nucleons.

Positron   An electron carrying a positive charge. The antiparticle sister to the electron.

Radiation pressure   The outward pressure of radiation emerging from the core of a star.

Radioactive decay   The disintegration and changing of a nucleus by the emission of a particle.

Red giant   A dying star that has exploded in the final stages of its life, forcing cool hydrogen outwards.

Strong nuclear force   The attractive force acting over a short range that is responsible for keeping the nucleons together.

Supernova   An unexpected violent explosion of a star resulting in a short-lived outburst of radiation.

Transmutation   The process of nuclear change that results in a nucleus changing from one element to another.

Answers to Ready to Study test

R1

(a) If atoms are thought of as hard spheres, when they are stacked in a regular pattern they will form smooth geometrical shapes, as shown in Figure 2.19.

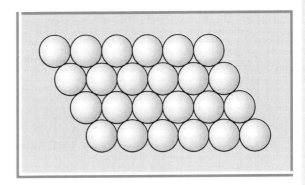

Figure 2.19   Answer to R1(a)

(b) The molecules of a leaking gas are moving very fast and continually changing direction because of collisions with molecules in the air. They therefore distribute themselves into all corners of their containing space. This is called diffusion.

R2

The nucleus of an atom is only about 1/10 000 the diameter of the whole atom and the electrons take up a negligible amount of space. So the volume taken up by the actual particles is a fraction of the atom's overall volume.

R3

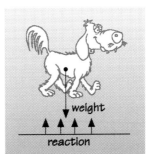

(a) See Figure 2.20.

(b) All the forces acting on the dog balance. There is no net force acting.

Figure 2.20   Answer to R3

(c)

Weight $= m \times g$

$$= 20\,\text{kg} \times 9.81\,\text{N}\,\text{kg}^{-1}$$

$$= 196.2\,\text{N}$$

$$= 2.0 \times 10^2\,\text{N} \text{ (to two significant figures)}$$

(d)

Change in gravitational potential energy

$$= mg\Delta h$$

$$= 196.2\,\text{N} \times 3.0\,\text{m}$$

$$= 588\,\text{J}$$

$$= 5.9 \times 10^2\,\text{J}$$

(to two significant figures)

R4

(a) A thick paper disposable glove would do.

(b) A heavy duty glove with a lead lining. (Tweezers or tongs should also be used in conjunction with these gloves. In reality the thickness of the glove needed would depend on the energies of the radiations.)

R5

The alpha particle would have greater kinetic energy because it has a much greater mass.

R6

Th and Pa refer to the chemical name of elements – you may recognize them as thorium and protactinium. 234 is the mass or nucleon number and 91 the atomic number of Pa. So this isotope of Pa has 91 protons and 143 neutrons (91 + 143 = 234). e is an electron, presumably emitted as a beta particle; it has no mass but carries a single negative charge.

R7

Stars: Sun, Betelgeuse, Proxima Centauri.

Planets: Jupiter, Earth, Pluto.

Galaxies: Milky Way, M100.

Answers to questions in the text

Q1

(a) It shows the order of the stops and which places are on the route. It gives relative distances and shows the terminal stops.

(b) It does not tell you the bus times, the actual route (the roads) or the fares.

Q2

(a) The hard spheres model shown in Figure 2.2(a). Hard spheres would bounce off each other at each collision, rather like billiard balls. The collision process would continue throughout the gas. The spheres would exert force on the walls of the gas container and so register the gas pressure.

(b) If you used a model of an atom based on the solar system then would the collision process continue after the first collision? If two solar systems were to collide the planets would smash together and disintegrate. There would certainly not be a clean collision with two solar systems emerging unscathed.

Q3

Your discussion may have covered questions such as 'What is a scientific fact?' and 'Do facts change with time?' You know that scientists use models and hypotheses to explain observations and make predictions, so you may have considered the relationship between these and 'facts' or 'the truth'. You will also be aware that these models and hypotheses are developed and improved (or discarded) all the time as new discoveries are made, so does this mean that the 'facts' are also changing? We hope you agreed that physics is not the static, unchanging subject, with no room for creativity, that the quoted student seems to think it is. That *would* be dull.

Q4

(a) The electrical force of attraction between proton and electron is given by

$$F = \frac{kq_1q_2}{r^2}$$

so

$$F = \frac{9.0 \times 10^9 \, \text{N m}^2 \, \text{C}^{-2} \times \left(1.6 \times 10^{-19} \, \text{C}\right)^2}{\left(1.0 \times 10^{-10} \, \text{m}\right)^2}$$

$$= 2.3 \times 10^{-8} \, \text{N}$$

$$\approx 10^{-8} \, \text{N}$$

(b) The electrical force is about 10^{40} times greater than the gravitational force between them.

Q5

The masses of planets, stars and galaxies are so great that their gravitational attraction becomes significant.

Q6

Charges can be separated on a small scale but on large scales the overall charges on a planet or star are balanced. Galaxies do not have a net positive or negative charge so there is no net electrical attraction or electrical repulsion.

Q7

The Coulomb force between the protons is

$$F = \frac{kq_1q_2}{r^2}$$

$$= \frac{9.0 \times 10^9 \, \text{N m}^2 \, \text{C}^{-2} \times \left(1.6 \times 10^{-19} \, \text{C}\right)^2}{\left(1.0 \times 10^{-14} \, \text{m}\right)^2}$$

$$= 2.304 \, \text{N}$$

$$= 2.3 \, \text{N (to two significant figures)}$$

The strong force will need to be at least this value, i.e. about 2 N.

Q8

$$E = mc^2$$

so

$$E = 1.26 \times 10^{-29} \, \text{kg} \times \left(3.0 \times 10^8 \, \text{m s}^{-1}\right)^2$$

$$= 1.1 \times 10^{-12} \, \text{J (to two significant figures)}$$

for one nucleon. So when four nucleons fuse the release of energy is $4.4 \times 10^{-12} \, \text{J}$.

Q9

Yes, plenty – about

$$1.0 \times 10^{26} \times 1.1 \times 10^{-12} \, \text{J} = 1.1 \times 10^{14} \, \text{J in fact.}$$

Q10

Yes, it could provide enough energy.

$$\frac{1.1 \times 10^{14} \, \text{J}}{7.0 \times 10^4 \, \text{J}} = 1.6 \times 10^9$$

so the energy from fusion of nuclei in a single cup of tea would be sufficient to make about 10^{10} cups of tea. This would be enough energy for Margie to keep brewing up for a period of time about equal to the age of Earth itself.

Q11

$$E = mc^2$$

$$= 5.0 \times 10^9 \, \text{kg} \times \left(3.0 \times 10^8 \, \text{m s}^{-1}\right)^2$$

$$= 4.5 \times 10^{26} \, \text{J}$$

This is the energy released every second, so the power output is

$$4.5 \times 10^{26} \, \text{J s}^{-1} = 4.5 \times 10^{26} \, \text{W}$$

Q12

$$\frac{2.0 \times 10^{30}\,\text{kg}}{5.0 \times 10^{9}\,\text{kg}\,\text{s}^{-1}} = 4.0 \times 10^{20}\,\text{s}$$

which is about 1.3×10^{13} years. So with more than 10^{13} years to go, there is no need to worry just yet.

Q13

(a) Using $E = mc^2$

$$E = 1.0 \times 10^{-30}\,\text{kg} \times \left(3.0 \times 10^{8}\,\text{ms}^{-1}\right)^2$$

$$= 9.0 \times 10^{-14}\,\text{J}$$

(b)

$$E = 9.0 \times 10^{-14}\,\text{J} \times \frac{6.02 \times 10^{23}}{0.235\,\text{kg}} \times 1.0\,\text{kg}$$

$$= 2.3 \times 10^{11}\,\text{J} \text{ (to two significant figures)}$$

Q15

(a) This is alpha decay, since the mass number decreases by 4 and the atomic number decreases by 2. So the emitted particle has a mass number of 4 and atomic number of 2, identifying it as doubly ionized helium (i.e. an alpha particle).

$$^{238}_{92}\text{U} \rightarrow\ ^{234}_{90}\text{Th} +\ ^{4}_{2}\text{He}$$

(b) The next radioactive decay is by beta emission since the mass number is unaltered but the atomic number increases by 1, showing that a nucleon change occurred, neutron to proton.

$$^{234}_{90}\text{Th} \rightarrow\ ^{234}_{91}\text{Pa} +\ ^{0}_{-1}\text{e}$$

Q16

The resulting nucleus has a mass number of $235 - 4 = 231$. The atomic number reduces by two to 90. It is in fact an isotope of thorium.

Q14

Type of radiation	Exactly what is it?	What are its properties?
Alpha	A fast-moving helium nucleus, two protons and two neutrons Carries a double positive charge	Intense trail of ionization lasting a few centimetres in air. Easily stopped by paper. Deflected by electric and magnetic fields
Beta	A fast-moving electron Carries a single positive or a single negative charge	Travels several metres in air Weaker trail of ionization Deflected by electric and magnetic fields
Gamma	A photon of electromagnetic radiation similar to an X-ray	Very penetrating. Stopped only by a centimetre thick shield of lead or several metres of concrete

Q17

At point M mass is 2.5 g (from 72 s to 144 s is a half-life time and therefore the mass halves from its value at 72 s). At point N mass is 1.25 g (from 144 s to 216 s is another 72 s interval).

Q18

In two half-lives the mass would reduce by $\frac{1}{2} \times \frac{1}{2}$. About 12.5 g of ^{234}Pa will be left.

Q19

(a) Remember to subtract the background count as shown in Table 2.3 before plotting the activity. Your graph should look like Figure 2.21.

(b) From the graph, half-life value is approximately 47 s.

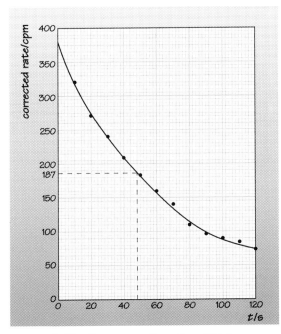

Figure 2.21 Answer to Question 19(a)

Q20

A graph of activity against time should give an age of about 12 000 years at 18 Bq activity.

Q21

The gap is the creation of combinations of elementary particles to form heavier elements, such as uranium, which are present in the Universe but were not created by the Big Bang. Supernovae provide the high temperature conditions necessary for particles to combine to undergo nucleosynthesis.

Q22

The scientists have found iron near the supernova in higher quantities than in our Sun.

Q23

We might include the following points in the article, you may be able to add some more of your own:

- extremes of conditions
- most stars we look at are stable, supernovae explode enabling us to see inside a star and observe nuclear processes taking place
- 'snapshots of ... stellar evolution'
- 'there is literally a little bit of a supernova inside all of us'
- production of the heavier elements
- supernovae are very bright so we can see them a long way off
- the supernova explosion was observed very shortly after it happened

Table 2.3 Radioactive decay of thoron gas corrected for background count

Time/s	10	20	30	40	50	60	70	80	90	100	110	120
Decay rate/cpm	346	297	265	234	208	185	165	133	122	114	104	98
Corrected rate/cpm	321	272	240	209	183	160	140	108	97	89	79	73

- this was the first direct evidence of core collapse, which was only postulated before
- it cleared up a lot of uncertainties
- the supernova is 100 000 times brighter than our Sun
- supernova explosions occur in our galaxy on average once in every 200 years, and we are long overdue one.

Q24

(a)

$$F = \frac{kq_1 q_2}{r^2}$$

$$= \frac{\left(9.0 \times 10^9 \, \text{Nm}^2 \, \text{C}^{-2}\right) \times \left(2 \times 1.6 \times 10^{-19} \, \text{C}\right)^2}{\left(2.0 \times 10^{-9} \, \text{m}\right)}$$

$$= 2.3 \times 10^{-10} \, \text{N} \text{ (to two significant figures)}$$

As the helium nuclei both carry positive charges, the force between them is repulsive

(b) At ten times the separation the force would be 1/100 times smaller.

(c)

Mass defect = 0.030376 units

$$= 5.04 \times 10^{-29} \, \text{kg}$$

therefore, as $E = mc^2$

$$E = 5.04 \times 10^{-29} \, \text{kg} \times \left(3.0 \times 10^8 \, \text{ms}^{-1}\right)^2$$

$$= 4.5 \times 10^{-12} \, \text{J}$$

to convert to eV

$$E = \frac{4.5 \times 10^{-12} \, \text{J}}{1.6 \times 10^{-19}}$$

$$= 28 \, \text{MeV}$$

Q25

(a) Fissile: A fissile nucleus is unstable and will respond to a neutron collision.

Non-fissile: A non-fissile nucleus will not break up when struck by a neutron.

(b) These are the mass numbers or nucleon numbers. They represent the total number of protons and neutrons in each nucleus.

(c) The Np nucleus will contain 93 protons and 239 nucleons.

(d) (i) The mass number remains 239. (ii) The atomic number increases by one to 94.

(e) They absorb the neutrons and so can control the amount of fission taking place.

Q26

(a) The brightness reached a maximum at day 2 and then reduced, rapidly at first and then more gradually.

(b) Radioisotopes will decay over time. The brightness shows a decay.

The rate of radioactive decay would be rapid at first and then die down in an exponential pattern. The graph shows a pattern that looks at first glance to be exponential.

(c) 18 million years ago.

(d) (i) A gamma-ray is a particle, a photon, of light of very short wavelength, about 10^{-14} m.

(ii) There would no change to the nuclear structure. Mass and atomic numbers would remain the same. Only the energy inside the nucleus would fall.

(e) (i) Probably very little. The Universe is unlikely to have changed so rapidly over the past 30 years. (ii) Recent technology, telescopes, photographic records and the increase in the number of interested observers would be the more likely reasons for more recorded supernovae sightings.

Q27

(a) There is confusion here about the term 'radiation'. The smoke detector uses a radioactive source that emits tiny particles. They travel only a few centimetres in air. Radiation from the Sun travels millions of miles through space and is a different form of radiation – it is rays of sunlight. The ultraviolet component of this radiation may cause cancer.

(b) The operator is frequently exposed to stray X-rays every day. They shield themselves from the accumulative effect. You receive a short dose only once. There is always some risk with exposure to X-rays, however your body does have a cell repair mechanism.

(c) There are no bombs in a nuclear power station. The small amount of uranium is kept in concrete shielded reactors with controls to avoid overheating.

(d) No. You cannot become radioactive by looking at a radioactive source. Only by touching an open source will you risk contamination. This will leave a small trace of radioisotope on your body and it will continue to irradiate you. In school only sealed sources are used.

Appendix 2.1 Understanding exponential processes

The most significant point about exponential processes is that the rate of change of a quantity at any time depends on the magnitude of the quantity at that time. If we think of rate of change as being the slope or gradient of a curve then when, for example, there are lots of nuclei available to decay the rate of decay will be high. With few nuclei remaining to decay the rate will be low. See Figure 2.22.

The relationship between the gradient and the quantity is summarized by the equation:

$$\frac{dN}{dt} = -\lambda N$$

The constant, λ, is called the decay constant. It represents the chance that a nucleus will disintegrate per second.

The minus sign shows that this is a decay process with the value of N gradually decreasing. It is possible for exponential processes to increase, in which case $\frac{dN}{dt}$ will be positive. This is seen in the equations describing the exponential growth of bacteria, for example.

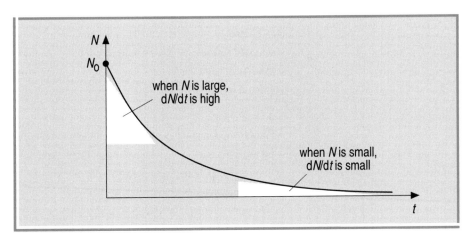

Figure 2.22 Radioactive decay

An equation relating N and t

To find a mathematical expression that accurately describes, or models, the radioactive decay process is not straightforward. $N = t$ will produce a straight line. $N = 3t^2$ will produce an increasing curve. $N = 1/t$ will give a curve with two asymptotes.

The expression that best models the reality of exponential decay is

$$N = N_0 e^{-\lambda t} \qquad (2.1)$$

This simply says that, after a time t, the number, N, of nuclei still to decay is a fraction of the original number of nuclei, N_0. The fraction (the minus sign ensuring it is always less than 1) is $e^{-\lambda t}$

As t increases this fraction will reduce and so the number of nuclei remaining will reduce. When $t = 0$ the fraction is 1 and this is the full number of nuclei, N_0, at the start. 'e' is a mathematical constant, rather like π. $e^{-\lambda t}$ is called an 'exponential function.'

The 'constant ratio' property of this process is more clearly seen when we consider the special case of the time taken for N to decrease to half its original value, i.e. from N_0 to $\dfrac{N_0}{2}$.

substituting $N = \dfrac{N_0}{2}$ in Equation (2.1) we

can show that

$$\frac{N_0}{2} = N_0 e^{-\lambda t}$$

or

$$0.5 = e^{-\lambda t}$$

Taking natural logs of both sides gives:

$$\ln 0.5 = -\lambda t$$

or

$$0.69 = \lambda t_{1/2}$$

The meaning of $t_{1/2}$

This particular time is called the 'half-life' of the decay process. It is the time taken for the number of nuclei to reduce to half its original value (N becomes $N_0/2$).

It is also the time for the 'activity' of the sample to reduce to half its original value.

In practice it is impossible for us to count individual nuclei, but we can use a ratemeter or counter to measure the rate of decay or 'activity'.

The time it takes for the activity to reduce to half its initial value is a measure of the half-life.

To determine the half-life of a sample it is good practice to take several pairs of readings from an activity–time graph. The mean value will give the half-life.

The world on an atomic scale is a strange place. Energy arrives in 'lumps' and particles behave like waves. Quantum theory is perhaps the most stunning development in twentieth-century physics. This section looks at how the light from stars can be modelled by simple 'black body' ideas and how an understanding of black-body radiation led people like Albert Einstein and Max Planck to explain the quantum revolution to the scientific world. The fact that light energy travels as lumps, called photons, has enabled science to understand and interpret the individual spectral fingerprint of all known elements. It is the information contained within the line spectra from stars that can tell us so much about temperatures, sizes and speed of motion of stars that are thousands of millions of miles away. Stars that we have no hope of getting close to in any way other than through the messages in their starlight.

READY TO STUDY TEST

Before you begin this section you should be able to:

- understand and apply the laws of reflection and refraction of light
- name the sequence of radiation in the electromagnetic spectrum
- understand the terms 'wavelength' and 'frequency' when applied to a wave
- discuss diffraction and interference of water waves
- understand that an atom may be divided into a nucleus and electrons
- calculate the kinetic energy and the momentum of a moving object
- use an ammeter and a voltmeter to measure current and potential difference.

QUESTIONS

R1 You probably look in a mirror at least once each day, perhaps to comb your hair. Draw a sketch to explain how you manage to see your reflection when you look into a mirror. You should draw the paths of rays of light and show the direction of these rays by means of arrows.

R2 Figure 3.1 shows light passing through a triangular prism.

(a) Explain what is happening to the light at the points where it enters and leaves the glass surface.

QUANTUM PHYSICS IN SPACE

(b) What happens to the wavelength and the frequency of the light?

(c) What happens to the speed and direction of the light?

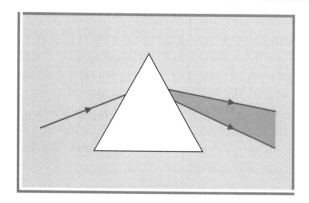

Figure 3.1 Light passing through a prism

R3 Here are some named parts of the electromagnetic spectrum: ultraviolet rays, radio waves, red light, X-rays.

(a) Arrange them in order of increasing wavelength, smallest first.

(b) Add one more member of the electromagnetic spectrum of your own choice in the correct place in the sequence.

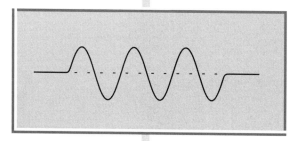

Figure 3.2
A wave travelling along a string

R4 Figure 3.2 shows a wave pattern of a wave made to travel along a string.

(a) Draw a sketch of a similar wave with a longer wavelength.

(b) Draw a sketch of a similar wave made by vibrating the string at a lower frequency.

R5 An archery arrow, mass 0.1 kg, was fired at a velocity of 20 m s^{-1}.

(a) Calculate (i) the momentum of the arrow, (ii) the kinetic energy of the arrow.

(b) Which of these quantities would double if the velocity of the arrow were to be 40 m s^{-1}?

R6 A frog sits on a lily pad behind a large rock in a still pond. A naughty child drops a stone in front of the rock creating waves of wavelength 0.045 m, which travel around the rock 0.26 m one way and 0.35 m the other before reaching the frog. How will these waves interact and what will be the effect on the frog?

3.1 Hot stars

Sir Isaac Newton spent a considerable amount of time wrestling with the nature of light. He is often shown in sketches holding a glass prism in the path of a beam of light. This in itself is not so remarkable, as most children find the chance to do something similar, but in 1665 Newton was one of the first scientists to make a study of a spectrum from the Sun. His interpretation of the apparently continuous rainbow of colours from blue through to red was based on the idea that the colours are already in the sunlight. He interpreted the spectrum as a display of the variety of colours that together form 'white' light. This was a very new idea at that time. Newton demonstrated that if pure red light shone through his prism no further colours appear.

Newton splitting white light into its various colours

Today we would say that the **refraction** of the white sunlight by the glass causes the colours to become **dispersed** into hues, each with its own distinct wavelength. The colours are already in the light – they are the light.

Some stars clearly show a hint of colour to observers on Earth, but it was not until 1863 that the Italian astronomer Angelo Secchi offered a crude categorization of stars by their different spectra.

 What technique do you think Angelo Secchi used to record the colours of stars in 1863? What instrumentation was at hand?

He would have had access to good telescopes. Although at this time the earliest black and white photographs were being pioneered they would be of no use to record the colours of stars. So, he probably simply used his own eye and telescope sightings.

A closer analysis of the energy of the Sun's spectrum shows that not all colours are represented with equal intensity and that radiation beyond the visible red and blue ends of the spectrum, infrared and ultraviolet, are also present. Figure 3.3(a) shows how the relative intensities of these radiations are represented in the Sun's spectrum.

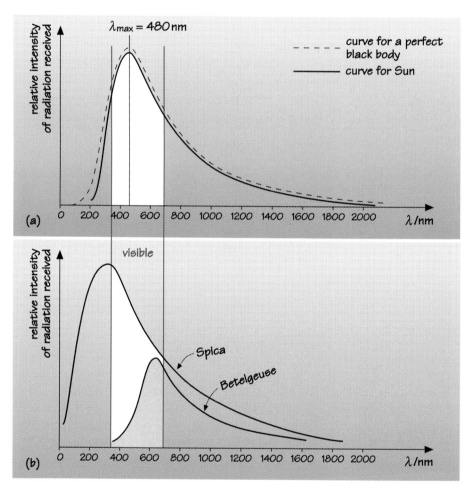

Figure 3.3 (a) Relative intensities for different wavelengths of the Sun's spectrum. (b) Relative intensities for different wavelengths of Spica's and Betelgeuse's spectra

For the Sun, the wavelength of radiation at which most energy is transmitted is in the visible part of the spectrum. For other stars, the spread of intensities favour the red end or blue end of the spectrum. You may have seen something similar looking at hot objects glowing in a flame. The colours of the object change as the temperature rises: from dull red, through bright red to white hot. The exact shape of the Sun's spread of wavelengths can be produced in the laboratory using a particular kind of object that radiates like a star. This type of object is known as a **black body**, and it absorbs all the radiation landing on it and radiates a continuous spectrum known as black-body radiation.

In the laboratory, a reasonable black body can be created from a hole in a box painted with a black interior. The radiation emerging from the hole will follow the black-body curve and will show a characteristic change as the temperature of the box is increased. At about 1300 K the hole will glow red hot. The temperatures of the stars are impossible to create in a laboratory so we have to extrapolate the theory of black-body radiation. We find that the temperatures have to reach 6000 K to radiate with a white glow. The Sun approximates to a perfect black body at 6000 K.

The radiation from hotter stars, for example Spica at 30 000 K (which appears blue/white), will show a similar shape but the maximum energy will be represented at a shorter wavelength. Cooler stars, such as Betelgeuse, surface temperature about 3500 K (which appears orange/red), will radiate more energy at longer wavelengths, as shown in Figure 3.3(b).

E Exploration 3.1 Simulating stars

40 MINUTES

Apparatus:

◆ four 12 V, 24 W lamps in holders
◆ one 1–5 A ammeter ◆ one 0–20 V voltmeter
◆ four power supplies (you could use 6 V mes lamps with battery packs)

Set up four 12 V, 24 W lamps at one end of a darkened room. Run them off separate power supplies and set the supplies to a range of potential differences from about 3 V to 12 V. Can you arrange for four distinctly different colours to be seen? Investigate the following:

(a) If each lamp represents a luminous star, which one is the hottest?

(b) Which one emits most energy per square metre of surface?

(c) Which would be a model for a red star and which for a white star?

(d) Use an ammeter and a voltmeter to measure the current and potential difference for each lamp. Multiply them to give a number that indicates the power output of each lamp.

(e) How many of the coolest lamps might you need to match the power of the hottest lamp?

(f) If these two extremes were stars, how much larger should the cool star be in order to match the brightness of the hot star?

In 1893 Wilhelm Wien proposed a relationship between the temperature of a black body and the wavelength having the maximum energy emission, λ_{max}. It is known as Wien's displacement law and can be used to calculate the surface temperature, T, of a star.

$$\lambda_{max}T = 2.9 \times 10^{-3}\ \text{m K}$$

The constant 2.9×10^{-3} m K is the result of Wien's experimental evidence. To ensure that the units of both sides of the equation balance, i.e. the equation is homogenous, the constant on the right-hand side has units of m × K.

Q1 The star Rigel, in the constellation of Orion the hunter, emits energy in the pattern of a black body. The wavelength emitting most energy is 240 nm, in the ultraviolet spectrum. Use this to calculate the surface temperature of Rigel. ◆

Q2 (a) Use Figure 3.3(a) to find the wavelength having the maximum energy. In which part of the electromagnetic spectrum does this wavelength lie?

(b) Use Wien's law to find a value for the surface temperature of the Sun.

(c) If this were the temperature of a black body what colour would the surface appear? ◆

Armed with Wien's law, physicists have calculated the temperatures of all the accessible stars in the region of our Sun. Einar Hertzsprung in Denmark in 1912 noticed that the hotter stars tended to be the brightest, and in 1913 Henry Norris Russell in the USA made a plot of the brightness and temperatures of all known stars. Such a plot is now known as the Hertzsprung–Russell (H–R) diagram and is shown in Figure 3.4.

Orion constellation showing Betelgeuse and Rigel

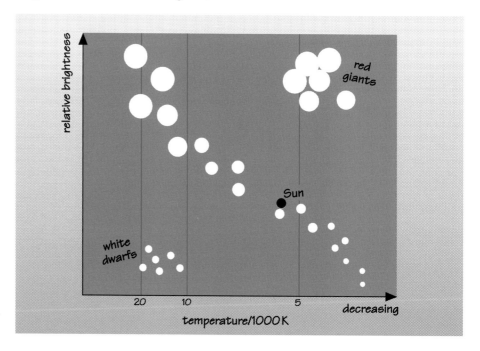

Figure 3.4
A simplified Hertzsprung–Russell diagram

Most stars lie on the 'main sequence', a band crossing the H–R diagram from the bottom right to the top left corners diagonally. However, there are some very cool but very bright stars to be seen. Such stars must be very large to be bright *and* cool; these are known as **red giants**. The class of small, hot stars in the lower left corner are **white dwarfs** and can be as small as Earth. The Sun is a main sequence star with a surface temperature of about 6000 K.

Stars are not constant in time. They have a birth and a death and during their life of about 1000 million years they will change colour from blue-white as they form to yellow-white during the greater part of their existence, often ending their days in a violent explosion resulting in a much larger and cooler red, dying star. The final collapse can lead to a tiny hot final phase before fading away into a rocky iron lump. So the red giants and white dwarfs in the H–R diagram are stars that are coming to the end of their lives. They are stars that have spent millions of years on the main sequence. Now at the end of their stellar life story they have either exploded to become cool red giants or have collapsed into hot white dwarfs.

 As it ages, will our Sun remain in the same place on the H–R diagram?

For most of its life the Sun will stay in the same position on the H–R diagram. However, in several million years the Sun will explode and become a red giant. It will then be placed elsewhere on the H–R plot. This will be temporary as the final fade away will create a hot white dwarf before oblivion and so the Sun will take up yet another position on the diagram.

Larger stars are likely to undergo one final supernova explosion, resulting in the ejection of gas and debris and the production of a tiny collapsing rocky remnant. Section 4 'Gravity and space' considers this in more detail. The end for these very largest stars with masses many thousand times that of the Sun is to progress beyond the last rocky stage. With such enormous mass the gravitational forces acting on the star itself will crush the star's rocky matter to such a degree that the interatomic forces will be overcome and the star's atomic structure will collapse. Such a star will be no more than a collection of nuclei, called a **neutron star**. (Figure 3.6 on page 57 shows the end stages in the lives of the Sun and a more massive star.)

3.2 Public science – quantum physics in space

The 1960s saw an explosion in television science fiction series in which Earth was contacted by creatures from space. Several of these were centred on radio-astronomy installations – modelled on Jodrell Bank, near Manchester, or the Mullard Observatory in Cambridge. In 'A for Andromeda', for example, radio signals from that fairly nearby galaxy gave scientists the blueprint for creating a woman ambassador for an advanced civilization located there – with terrifying consequences.

Imagine, then, the excitement when a regularly pulsed radio signal from space was first detected. And this was not a signal from Andromeda, but from within our own galaxy – in astronomical terms, on our own doorstep. Also, the signal had been picked up, not by a grey-haired professor, but by a young post-graduate student during a routine programme to scan the skies and collect data for her PhD thesis.

SCIENCE REPORT

ASTRONOMY

More about pulsating stars

By Nature-Times News Service

Less than two months after the announcement of the discovery of pulsating radio signals from space, astronomers met yesterday at the Royal Astronomical Society to discuss how they are to be explained. The importance scientists attach to the signals was emphasized by the number of theories put forward and the urgency with which astronomers are training their radio telescopes on the sources. Many of the details presented at the symposium also appear in a series of articles in the current issue of *Nature*, published today.

The meeting was one of the most crowded that the Royal Astronomical Society has had recently, and several astronomers had to watch proceedings on closed-circuit television.

According to Dr. A. G. Lyne and Professor Graham Smith of Jodrell Bank, the vibrations making up the radio waves from the pulsating sources are confined, to a greater or lesser extent, to one direction. Vibrations characteristic of radio waves are normally at all directions at right angles to the direction of the beam, but there are cases when radio waves from space favour vibrations in one direction.

This new characteristic of the pulsating signals is called linear polarization. The importance of this discovery, announced by Professor Graham Smith at yesterday's meeting, is that it can yield information about the way the pulsating signals are emitted.

So far four sources of pulsating signals have been found, but astronomers do not rule out that there may be several more. Three of them emit pulses at intervals of a little more than one second. A fourth – likely to receive a great deal of attention from astronomers – pulsates at quarter-second intervals. The intervals between pulses are maintained with amazing accuracy – the most remarkable feature of the signals.

Astronomers say that the discovery of pulsating signals is as important as the discovery of quasars six years ago. It is certain that an entirely new class of object has been discovered.

Dr. A. Hewish and his colleagues at Cambridge University, who discovered the signals, suggested that they may come from very dense stars which are vibrating. According to the Cambridge group, white dwarf stars or, more probably, neutron stars are likely candidates. Neutron stars are thought to be the final stage in the evolution of stars such as the sun, out so far they have escaped detection. This is one reason why the pulsating signals are causing so much excitement.

Dr. Lyne and Professor Graham Smith say this theory cannot account for the linear polarization observed at Jodrell Bank. They also doubt the theory put forward by Dr. W. C. Saslaw, Dr. J. Faulkner, and Dr. P. A. Strittmatter of Cambridge University on the same grounds.

Dr. Saslaw and his colleagues, writing in *Nature* a fortnight ago (*Science Report,* March 29), suggested that the signals may come from double star systems comprising two neutron stars orbiting around each other. Because neutron stars are so dense, each star acts rather like a lens. focusing radio waves

As the new findings filtered out into the astrophysical community, theorists worked overtime to try to explain the signals the observers were picking up on their radio dishes. They quickly ruled out the 'Little Green Men' hypothesis – the idea that we were being contacted from space – but they experienced considerable difficulties coming up with a reasonable explanation. You can get some idea of the ferment by reading the report of a meeting of the Royal Astronomical Society, carried in *The Times* on 11 April 1968, reproduced below.

Q3 What types of astronomical object did the various astronomers mentioned in the article think might be responsible for producing the pulsed radio signals that were observed?

(*Hint:* The candidates for explaining these signals seem to depend either on pulsing or rotating radio signals, although there are variations on the themes. Don't be surprised that, this early in the understanding of the signals, the scientists do not agree with one another and that no explanation seems without its flaws.) ◆

SCIENCE REPORT

emitted by active regions – like solar flares – on the other.

The two stars are like a lighthouse – each time the beam flashes across the earth a radio pulse is received. This means that the pulses come alternately from the two stars. An argument against this explanation is a study by Dr. Scott and Mr. Collins of Cambridge, who have found no evidence that alternate pulses are any different.

The two scientists at Jodrell Bank say measurements with the 250ft. radio telescope show that each pulse contains several components, each with a different characteristic direction of vibration. They suggest that the signals come from regions that are very small by astronomical standards – at least one dimension must be less than 10cm. and magnetic fields must be involved to explain the linear polarization.

How was the polarization measured? Two small radio aerials were fixed at right angles at the focus of the parabolic dish of the radio telescope. Each aerial was sensitive to radio waves polarized in one direction. By looking at the strength of the pulses picked up in receivers connected to each aerial the extent of polarization of the signals can be judged.

The quarter-second repetition interval of one of the sources – designated CP 0950, where CP stands for Cambridge pulsating source and the figure indicates its position in the sky – is significant. Professor Fred Hoyle and Dr. J. Narlikar, of the Institute of Theoretical Astronomy at Cambridge, write in this week's *Nature* that periods as short as a quarter-of-a-second can only just be accounted for by a vibrating white dwarf star. The agreement is "uncomfortably tight", however. This is particularly so because the receivers at Cambridge that measured the signals are not able to detect appreciably shorter periods anyway.

The amplitudes of the pulses vary a great deal, difficult to understand when the timing of the pulses seems to be controlled so precisely. Professor Hoyle and Dr. Narlikar suggest that this can be explained if the signals are connected with exploding stars called supernovae.

Supernovae explosions are thought to be triggered by nuclear reactions in certain kinds of star. in certain circumstances the dispersed material may collapse together again because of gravity forces. The collapsed material may "bounce"

back to something like its original size.

What do the pulsating stars look like? So far there seems to be no certain answer to this. Dr. J. A. Bailey and Dr. C. D. Mackay have used the Cambridge radio telescope to measure an accurate position for the object with the quarter-second period, CP 0950. They compared this position with photographs of the sky taken with the optical telescope on Mount Palomar in the United States.

They found a very faint red star near the position of the source of the radio signals, but the accuracy of the radio position is not good enough to make the identification certain. There is no bright object that could be associated with the signals. Clearly, whatever is producing the pulsating emissions must be very faint. This is compatible with the neutron star hypothesis.

Another pulsating source, CP 1919, has been almost certainly identified with a faint yellow star, a rather unusual object having no prominent spectral lines.

(*The Times*, 11 April 1968)

Jocelyn Bell Burnell

Q4 Astronomers supporting one of the possible candidates said the 'agreement is "uncomfortably tight"'. What do you think they meant? ◆

The student who discovered the first **pulsar** signals was Jocelyn Bell Burnell, now Professor of Astronomy at the Open University. The first pulsar was discovered in 1967, and several months of checking were needed before the results could be made public. Here Professor Bell Burnell explains how she made the discovery of pulsars and their significance for astronomy.

Interview with Professor Jocelyn Bell Burnell

Before their discovery, no one had predicted that some types of stars would produce pulsed radio signals. So, if you weren't actually looking for them, how was it you found these pulsars?

The project I was working on was to map all the sky visible from our observatory in Cambridge, looking for quasars. Quasars are very distant objects, very powerful, and – in a radio telescope – they would show up as objects that 'twinkled'. As well as identifying these quasars we could also see how large they were on the sky – their angular diameter. So you can see that we had very distant horizons. And so we were not expecting things on our own doorstep – within our own galaxy – to pop up and start waving at us.

At that time, the output from the telescope was in the form of a roll of chart paper with a trace from a pen all along it. And we saw these regular pulses, at about one every half a second. Now that was very unexpected. So after we picked up the first of these traces in 1967, we spent a long time checking our equipment to make sure there was nothing that could be accounting for these pulses. And we checked things like local interference to make sure that wasn't the source of our signal. In all we spent several months working through all the possibilities that could have accounted for our pulsed signal, until about Christmas 1967 we were sure that it was something 'out there' that was responsible.

All this time the telescope had been producing rolls of chart paper at about 100 feet per day. I was working on these charts every spare moment I had, but – by Christmas 1967 – a backlog of about half a mile had built up. Then, on 21 December, we found the second pulsar in our data. That really was the 'eureka' moment – the moment when you feel like leaping naked from the bath and running down the road, you're so excited – because the second pulsar we saw came from a very different part of the sky from the first. And that, in turn, suggested that there would be many more pulsars and we were only looking at the tip of the iceberg.

So, having found the first pulsar, and then 'confirmed' it by detecting the second, what explanations did you have for this type of signal?

When the first one had come through we had jokingly labelled it LGM, standing for 'Little Green Men'. Radio astronomers were keenly aware that, if there were civilizations out there, then the most likely means of contact they would try would be by radio. But we were very tongue-in-cheek about this LGM label since the signalling technique being used was a very stupid one. The pulses were regular in frequency, but modulated in amplitude (**amplitude modulated**), rather than **frequency modulated** as would be the sensible approach. So it meant if our signal was due to an external civilization, it was a pretty stupid one.

When we got the second pulsar, it was clear we were not being contacted. Otherwise you would have had to assume that *two* civilizations in totally different parts of the galaxy had, at one and the same time, decided to contact one insignificant planet using the same – very stupid – technique. So that really did squash any lingering doubts about little green men.

But we were still left with the problem of what this was. We were certain now that we were witnessing a naturally occurring phenomenon 'out there' but we did not have a good physical explanation for what we were seeing. So during that first few months there was an awful lot of 'theorizing on the hoof'. We did, however, have a couple of helpful suggestions.

The first was the idea that there could be very dense neutron stars, which could spin fast, possibly emitting radio waves. Then there was a paper in the journal *Nature* by Franco Pacini in the middle of 1967 – remarkably prophetic – suggesting that the Crab nebula might be powered by a strong emitter of radiation. But there were other ideas too, that you could have pulsating white dwarf stars: stars which were not completely solid but had an atmosphere. And I can remember that we had a real semantic discussion when we were writing our paper. Were we looking at pulsed stars, pulsating stars or pulsing stars?

But finally the idea that these pulsars were spinning neutron stars, with a 'lighthouse beam' of radio waves coming from them, came through as the explanation for these pulsars.

These are clearly rather odd objects. Where exactly do pulsars fit into the life cycle of stars?

Pulsars are a form of life after death for stars which originally were some twenty times as massive as the Sun. These stars go through a catastrophic supernova explosion, in which the core of the star collapses and reaches the density of an atomic nucleus. One of the most significant things about them, in my view, is that they make **black holes** seem much more feasible. From a neutron star pulsar to a black hole is just one more step. As well as pulsars

which pulse on the timescale of a fraction of a second, you get ones spinning much faster, a thousand times a second. These are a form of life after life after death, and there is much active research into just how these work.

Although the first claim of planets around this type of pulsars was withdrawn, the results from the Arecibo observatory in Puerto Rico, I think, are pretty solid. But these planets are not going to have life on them. Every time the pulsar spins they are going to be bathed in a lethal beam of radiation. If you had a pulsar like that in our Moon, I once worked out that you could put a steak at the focus of the Jodrell Bank radio dish and flash fry it, the radiation is so intense. And that's just in the radio wavelength. Some of these pulsars have X-ray pulses as well.

You have clearly established a formidable reputation internationally as a research astronomer. But, certainly in Britain, there are not many women who have made a successful career in astronomy at the present time. Why do you think this might be?

Astronomy actually does better in terms of the number of women involved in it than, say, physics. It probably does better than most of the physical sciences. And since the route into astronomy is often through physics, it is clear that the relatively low numbers of women in astronomy is nothing to do with the intellectual demands the subject makes.

What I find interesting is the enormous variation country by country. If you look at France, Italy, Mexico, Argentina, Eastern Europe, then you are getting up to 40% of astronomers being women. But in Britain, Germany, the USA, for example, the percentage is rather smaller. It has a lot to do with culture, in my view, rather than intellectual ability. Maybe there is something about being British, about our work ethic and what we expect, what is 'appropriate' for British women, that is the problem.

E ▸ Exploration 3.2 Discovering pulsars

20 MINUTES

Put yourself into Professor Bell Burnell's shoes in 1967 when, as a student, she first detected a pulsar signal. What would your reactions be to this and what would you do?

So, before 1967 neutron stars were no more than a twinkle in the eye of theoretical astronomers. But that year Jocelyn Bell Burnell and Anthony Hewish, working in Cambridge, detected the regular-as-clockwork pulses from what was later known to be a pulsating neutron star – a pulsar. Spinning stars speed up as they collapse rather like the spin of an ice-skater when pulling in their arms. In physics we interpret this by saying that a rotating body conserves its **angular momentum**. The angular momentum of a neutron star remains constant as it collapses and so the rate of spin increases. Appendix 4.1 at the end of Section 4 deals with angular momentum.

In a spinning pulsar, particles are accelerated along the directions of the star's magnetic field, resulting in electromagnetic radiation emerging from the north and south magnetic poles. In this sense the pulsar then acts rather like a lighthouse beacon spraying radiation into space at regular 1.337 s intervals with each pulse of radiation lasting 0.3 s. This is what Jocelyn Bell Burnell and Anthony Hewish detected. See Figure 3.5.

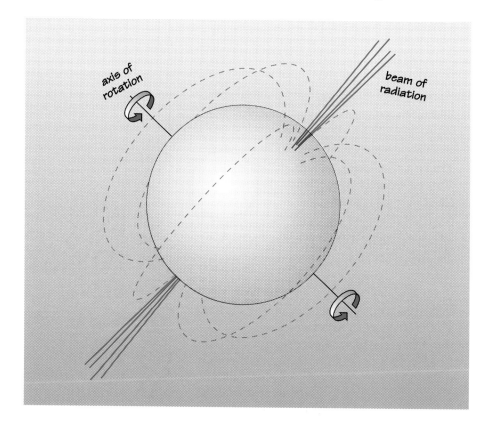

Figure 3.5
Radiation from a spinning pulsar

If the gravitational physics remains unchanged under such conditions, it is theoretically possible for the enormous forces to crush even nuclei together. Such a collapsed star is difficult to imagine. It would occupy a tiny point but the mass of a teaspoon of such material would be millions of millions of tonnes. Its gravity would become so intense that it would attract all matter in its locality, so fuelling the inexorable crushing effect.

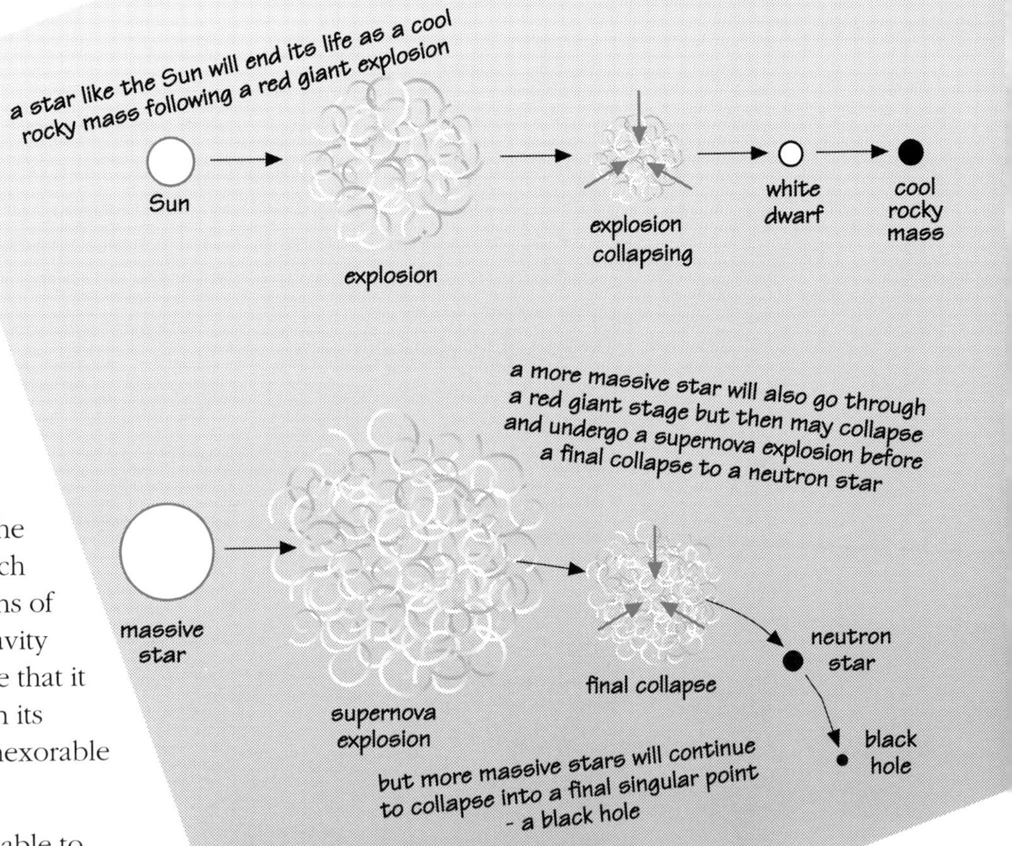

Not even light would be able to overcome such gravitational force. Nothing would emerge from this single point. It would be a **cosmic singularity**, a black hole. (See Figure 3.6.) The word 'singularity' in physics is used whenever an event is proposed that marks the start or end of a process and the exact understanding of what happens beyond the event is unclear.

a star like the Sun will end its life as a cool rocky mass following a red giant explosion

Sun

explosion

explosion collapsing

white dwarf

cool rocky mass

a more massive star will also go through a red giant stage but then may collapse and undergo a supernova explosion before a final collapse to a neutron star

massive star

supernova explosion

final collapse

neutron star

but more massive stars will continue to collapse into a final singular point – a black hole

black hole

Figure 3.6
Final scenes from the death of a star depend on the amount of matter in the star

Scientists are rarely happy with theories that produce singularities. They seem to lead to a dead end with no way out. In the case of a black hole the obvious questions like 'where does all the mass go to?' are not at all easy to digest. Science fiction has had a field day with black holes. There have been suggestions that black holes will lead to parallel universes and that perhaps by moving through a black hole you can experience time travel. It is interesting to note that theoretical physics is starting to produce ideas that are not wildly different from the science fiction stories of twenty years ago. The concept of a space–time wormhole that links two parts of the Universe is a serious theoretical concept.

 If light cannot escape from a black hole, what is the evidence that black holes do exist?

The evidence is from their effect on material in other nearby stars and galaxies. The accelerating material from these stars, which is attracted towards a black hole, gives off X-rays as it disappears beyond the **event horizon**. It is this radiation that is detected.

3.3 The quantum revolution

The characteristic black-body radiation curve shown in Figure 3.3 is the result of actual measurements. Such results are described as empirical (found by doing experiments). But when theoretical physicists tried to explain the shape of the curve they found that their conventional physics just wasn't good enough. The best match between theory and practice was produced by Rayleigh and Jeans in 1900 and was a good fit at long wavelengths (see Figure 3.7). However, it could not predict the observed maximum shape of the distribution of energies from a black body. In fact it predicted the opposite behaviour at short wavelengths – a situation that became known as the ultraviolet catastrophe.

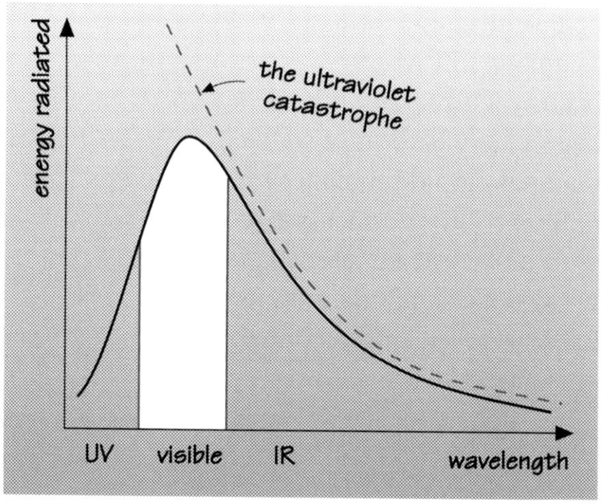

Figure 3.7
Rayleigh and Jeans's experimental results

At the beginning of the twentieth century it was thought that an amount of energy was 'continuous'; that is, that it could be divided up infinitely often. Against this background Max Planck proposed the bold and novel idea that energy came in indivisible lumps, much as matter comes in indivisible lumps called atoms. These may also be referred to as discrete packets but their correct name is quanta (one packet is called a **quantum**). Any energetic system, according to Planck, would therefore have either one, two, three, etc., quanta of energy. Using this approach Planck perfectly explained the shape of the black-body radiation curves by allowing oscillating molecules in a hot black body to have energy of n units of quanta. His revolutionary idea of 'quantum theory' was received with some opposition from the traditional physics community. However, when, in 1905, Einstein used a parallel idea, that of light quanta, to explain the **photoelectric effect**, the world view of energy was forced to change.

Photoelectric effect

In the photoelectric effect, light incident on a cleaned metal surface can result in electrons being 'knocked out' of the metal. We call these electrons **photoelectrons**, simply to describe their place of origin; they are just the same as other electrons. It was noticed that this effect happened only at frequencies of light higher than a minimum frequency. This is called the **threshold frequency**. For zinc, this threshold

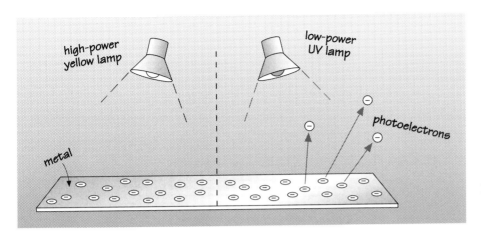

Figure 3.8
Photoelectrons being ejected

frequency is in the violet end of the visible spectrum. At lower frequencies, yellow light for example, no photoelectrons are emitted from the zinc, not even when the power of the yellow light is increased ten-fold or more. Yet with an ultraviolet source of low power the photoelectrons emerge. This is illustrated in Figure 3.8.

20 MINUTES

E Exploration 3.3 The photoelectric effect

Apparatus:

◆ Gold-leaf electroscope ◆ ultraviolet light source
◆ 12 V, 24 W lamp ◆ polythene rod ◆ flat piece of zinc
◆ emery paper ◆ duster ◆ crocodile clip ◆ 4 mm plug

Take care not to look directly at a ultraviolet lamp. Ultraviolet light can severely damage your eyes.

Clean the surface of the piece of zinc with the emery paper. Attach the zinc to the metal cap of the gold-leaf electroscope using the crocodile clip and the 4 mm plug. Using the polythene rod and the duster, rub the rod and charge up the electroscope by touching the zinc or the cap. You should see that the leaf will be deflected. Now bring an ultraviolet light source near to the zinc. You should notice that the leaf deflection reduces. This is the photoelectric effect in action. The electrons are being ejected from the zinc by photons of ultraviolet light. The leaf is losing charge and so falling. Repeat the experiment using a white light source, perhaps a 12 V, 24 W lamp. Does the leaf behave in the same way as before? Einstein received a Nobel prize for his explanation of this behaviour.

Einstein proposed that the energy of light arrived in quantified units, each one, called a photon, carrying a 'packet' of energy proportional in size to the frequency of the light. This packet of energy, E, is equal to a constant, h, times the frequency, f, of the light.

$$E = hf$$

where h is Planck's constant, 6.6×10^{-34} J s.

The photoelectrons with greatest energy would be those emitted from near the metal surface (Figure 3.9). A certain threshold energy had to be delivered to free the electrons from a surface. This was called the **work function** of the metal, Φ. A liberated electron gets the whole amount of energy in the quantum. Once it was liberated from the surface, any remaining energy was left as kinetic energy of the liberated photoelectrons E_{Kmax}. Relating this to the energy of a single photon we can say:

$$hf = \Phi + E_{Kmax}$$

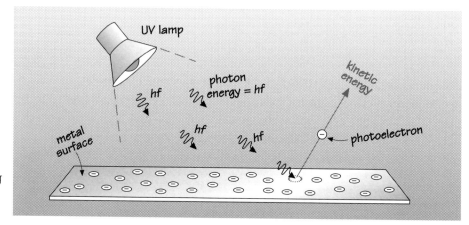

Figure 3.9
Photoelectrons being ejected with some kinetic energy

Slower-moving photoelectrons would be those that had interacted with a photon at a place below the metal surface. These photoelectrons would have expended some of their kinetic energy to reach the surface. They will emerge with a reduced velocity.

It is relatively easy to collect photoelectrons and register their presence on a sensitive ammeter (see Figure 3.10). By giving the electron collector a negative potential it is possible to reduce the photoelectron current by repelling all but the fastest electrons. At a higher negative potential even the fastest photoelectrons don't manage to cross the gap to the collector.

The potential difference that achieves this 'null' result is known as the stopping potential, V_S. When even the fastest photoelectrons have been

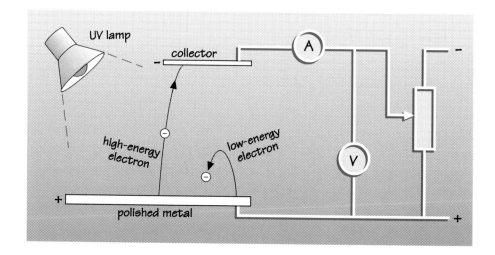

Figure 3.10
Experimental arrangement to collect photoelectrons

repelled completely it is correct to say that their initial kinetic energy has been transformed into potential energy in the electric field.

Electric PE = $E_{K\text{max}}$, so for photoelectrons with charge q

$$qV_s = E_{K\text{max}}$$

Q5 The stopping potential required for a photoelectric demonstration was found to be –6.5 V. Calculate the maximum kinetic energy of the photoelectrons. (The charge on an electron is -1.6×10^{-19} C.) ◆

Q6 If in the previous example the frequency of radiation incident on the photoelectric material has been 0.88×10^{16} Hz, calculate a value for the work function of the metal surface. ◆

It was by considering light to be photons that Einstein managed to explain the photoelectric effect. You may be forgiven for struggling with this new idea. Max Planck said that anyone who is not puzzled by the ideas of quantum theory doesn't understand the ideas! It requires a new way of thinking about energy and it is intellectually challenging.

So, where do you stand when asked the question: 'is light a wave or a particle?' A confident physicist in the twentieth century would respond something like:

> 'Well it is both and neither. It depends on the context of the question. If the light in question is liberating electrons from the surface of a metal then it is behaving like a particle. If it is producing an interference pattern through a grating then it is behaving like a wave.'

The skill of a good physicist is to select a model that best suits the situation.

 If what we have traditionally thought of as a wave, light, can be also considered a particle, is the reverse possible? Can things which are considered particles be treated as if they behaved like waves? Does a tomato have a wavelength for example?

The answer is yes. Following the next section you should be able to calculate its value.

The French scientist Louis de Broglie, in 1926, proposed that all particles have an associated wavelength. He gave the relationship between the particle's momentum, p, and the wavelength as:

$$p = \frac{h}{\lambda}$$

where h is Planck's constant, 6.6×10^{-34} J s.

PRINCE LOUIS DE BROGLIE (1892–1987)

Prince Louis de Broglie was of noble descent, his ancestors having served French monarchs since the time of Louis XIV. He was awarded the 1929 Nobel Prize for physics for 'his discovery of the wave nature of electrons'.

The experimental evidence to support de Broglie came from electrons. When fired at a thin graphite target, electrons were seen to produce interference rings caused by the **diffraction** of the electrons. Diffraction is explained in Section 5 'Light in space'. When waves pass through small gaps of a similar size to the wavelength of the waves they spread out. This is called diffraction. Two or more such gaps will cause the diffracted waves through each gap to overlap and interfere with each other. As a result, some waves will meet others and cancel out while others will meet and add up. The result is a pattern of bright and dark interference fringes. It was just such a set of fringes that were seen when electrons passed through a thin graphite film.

So electrons became part of the new way of looking at matter and waves. Known as **wave–particle duality**, this feature of quantum physics is a modern but well established idea.

 If a tomato, mass 200 g is thrown at 20 m s^{-1} from an angry crowd, what will its wavelength be? Will its diffraction be noticed as it passes though a line of policemen spaced 0.5 m apart?

The momentum, p, of the tomato is given by $p = \text{mass} \times \text{velocity}$.

Using

$$p = \frac{b}{\lambda}$$

we get

$$\lambda = \frac{b}{p}$$

$$= \frac{b}{m \times v}$$

$$= \frac{6.6 \times 10^{-34} \text{ J s}}{0.200 \text{ kg} \times 20 \text{ m s}^{-1}}$$

$$= 1.65 \times 10^{-34} \text{ m}$$

$$= 1.7 \times 10^{-34} \text{ m (to two significant figures)}$$

Diffraction is noticed only when the gap spacing is of the same order as the particle wavelength. With a spacing of 0.5 m, the policemen are just a shade too far apart for the wave property of the tomato to be noticed!

Q7 At CERN (a particle accelerator in Geneva) protons, mass 1.7×10^{-27} kg, are accelerated to a speed of 1.2×10^8 m s^{-1}. Calculate their momentum, p, and their de Broglie wavelength, λ, at this speed. ◆

In just a short space of time a simple and elegant idea of energy being 'lumpy' managed to revolutionize physics. But the beginning of the twentieth century was a time of revolution. Radioactivity had just been discovered, Thomson had recently discovered the electron, Rutherford was about to discover the atomic nucleus and particles were about to be waves. Astronomers, however, still thought that the Sun was at the centre of the Milky Way, which was the Universe! This also was all about to change.

3.4 The coded messages in spectral lines

Newton had shown the existence of spectral colours in sunlight as early as 1665, when he was only 23. However, it was not until the nineteenth century that scientists made the next new discoveries. Their light came from sources of different colours, such as a candle flame or a hot filament, and when passed through a narrow slit and prism light from these sources did not always give the full continuous spectrum of colours. In 1802, William Wollaston first noticed dark lines in these spectra. He realized that these were not simply gaps between colours. Certain wavelengths of light were conspicuous by their absence from the spectrum. This is called an **absorption spectrum** because the colours have been absorbed and removed from the light during its passage through the cooler gases around the flames. On the other hand when an excited gas glows, an **emission spectrum** can be recorded with exactly the same colours present as were missing from the absorption spectrum. Hence an absorption and an emission spectrum are complementary – rather like two pieces of a jigsaw puzzle. See Figure 3.11.

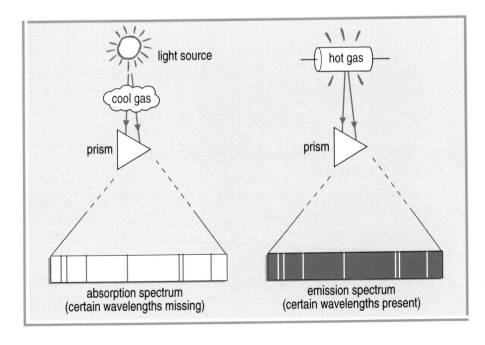

Figure 3.11
Absorption and emission spectra

Exploration 3.4 Observing spectral lines

 (30 MINUTES)

 Commercial gas discharge tubes use high-voltage supplies. Take care not to touch contacts in the supplies.

Apparatus:

◆ hand-held spectroscope ◆ potassium permanganate (potassium manganate VII) crystals (oxidizing and harmful) ◆ glass beaker ◆ 12 V lamp in holder ◆ commercial gas-filled tubes ◆ suitable power supply

You can explore absorption and emission spectra using a hand-held spectroscope. For emission spectra, find some brightly coloured lamps and observe them in a dim room. The red neon 'on' indicators on some power supplies will be a good source of red and yellow line spectra. Commercially available discharge tubes will show the emission lines for hydrogen, mercury, neon and other gases.

For absorption spectra, you might like to try the following. Set up a 12 V lamp about 1 m away from your spectroscope. Place a glass or plastic container containing a coloured liquid between you and the lamp. Potassium permanganate solution is one possible liquid. You might like to try coloured dyes in water, perhaps a chemical indicator in a slightly acidic solution. Cola or orange drinks might also reveal missing colours. Observing the spectrum of the lamp with the beaker will reveal missing colours. Observing the spectrum of the lamp without the beaker will show a bright continuous spectrum. The presence of the coloured solution should show up as dark bands where particular colours have been absorbed.

 Calculate the frequency of red light of wavelength 655 nm.

$$f = \frac{c}{\lambda}$$

$$= \frac{3.0 \times 10^8 \, \text{ms}^{-1}}{655 \times 10^{-9} \, \text{m}}$$

$$= 4.58 \times 10^{14} \, \text{Hz}$$

$$= 4.6 \times 10^{14} \, \text{Hz (to two significant figures)}$$

 An emission spectrum of a gas contained the following three frequencies of light:

$f_1 = 4.75 \times 10^{14}$ Hz
$f_2 = 5.03 \times 10^{14}$ Hz
$f_3 = 5.30 \times 10^{14}$ Hz

Calculate the wavelengths of light, in nm, missing from the absorption spectrum of the same gas (give the answers to two significant figures).

For each frequency the corresponding wavelength can be found

using $\lambda = \dfrac{c}{f}$

$$\lambda_1 = \frac{3.0 \times 10^8 \text{ m}}{4.75 \times 10^{14} \text{ Hz}}$$

$$= 6.316 \times 10^{-7} \text{ m}$$

$$= \left(6.316 \times 10^{-7} \times 1 \times 10^9 \right) \text{nm}$$

$$= 6.3 \times 10^2 \text{ nm or } 630\text{nm}$$

$$\lambda_2 = \frac{3.0 \times 10^8 \text{ m}}{5.03 \times 10^{14} \text{ Hz}}$$

$$= 5.964 \times 10^{-7} \text{ m}$$

$$= \left(5.964 \times 10^{-7} \times 1 \times 10^9 \right) \text{nm}$$

$$= 6.0 \times 10^2 \text{ nm or } 600\text{nm}$$

$$\lambda_3 = \frac{3.0 \times 10^8 \text{ m}}{5.30 \times 10^{14} \text{ Hz}}$$

$$= 5.660 \times 10^{-7} \text{ m}$$

$$= \left(5.660 \times 10^{-7} \times 1 \times 10^9 \right) \text{nm}$$

$$= 5.7 \times 10^2 \text{ nm or } 570\text{nm}$$

What was even more significant in Wollaston's discovery was the fact that the particular spectral line pattern seemed to characterize a particular source of light. The missing wavelengths in an absorption spectrum gave the clue to the identity of the cool gas absorbing the light. The colours present in an emission spectrum were a 'fingerprint' that perfectly characterized a hot gas. Spectral physics became a subject whereby the exact nature of an unknown gas could be determined simply by analysing the absorption or emission spectrum. A spectral scientist could look at a spectrum and immediately identify the element responsible for producing it, rather like you would be able to recognize a member of your family from a holiday snapshot. (See Figure 3.12 overleaf.)

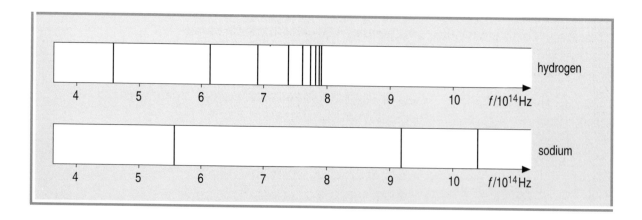

Figure 3.12
Spectra of hydrogen
and sodium

A spectral message from the Sun

It was Joseph Fraunhofer who in 1814 first recorded missing wavelengths in the Sun's spectrum. He noticed, in particular, that two lines in the yellow part of the spectrum corresponded exactly to two yellow lines present in the spectrum of sodium in the laboratory. Fraunhofer labelled these the sodium 'D' lines.

The German physicist Gustav Kirchhoff gave the first clear explanation of this:

> the rays of light which form the solar spectrum have passed through the vapour of sodium and have thus suffered the absorption which the vapour of sodium must exert.

> (Kirchhoff, 1859, p. 662, translated by Roscoe, 1870, p. 217)

This discovery was quickly followed by matching other sets of lines in the Sun's spectrum with known chemical spectra, revealing the presence of iron, calcium and magnesium in the Sun. So, during this period in the nineteenth century the chemical constituents of a star were being revealed through the messages in spectra and, perhaps more significantly, it was beginning to look as if space consisted of the same matter as Earth.

 Might it have been possible for spectral scientists to discover a completely new element in space that was not known about on Earth? How would it have been recognized?

A spectrum might be found that had no known counterpart on Earth. It might be a brand new element that exists only in space. If this were to be the case then Earth would not be made of the same matter as space. Discuss with others in your group why this could pose some problems for cosmologists.

The English astronomer Norman Lockyer observed the spectrum from the outer rim of the Sun during the total eclipse in 1865. The missing lines in this spectrum revealed the presence of hydrogen gas. We now know that

99% of the entire Universe is hydrogen gas. By the late 1860s William Huggins in London had successfully photographed stellar line spectra and so established stellar spectroscopy as the main tool for understanding what stars are made of.

The practical value to astronomers of spectral information has been established. But what did the theoretical physicists make of spectral lines? The answer, in a nutshell, is not much at all, certainly not during the exciting days of the nineteenth century when the techniques of stellar spectroscopy were being developed. At this time physicists had no mechanism that could successfully explain the production of line spectra.

In 1885, Johann Balmer, a mathematics teacher, saw that the visible lines in the spectrum of hydrogen gas could be fitted to a mathematical pattern, but he had no justification for the pattern other than it seemed to fit the lines. Physics had to wait until after the turn of the century for an explanation, when Niels Bohr (a Danish physicist) used the quantum theory of Planck and Einstein to produce a new and revolutionary model of an atom in 1913. Bohr's model is illustrated in Figure 3.13.

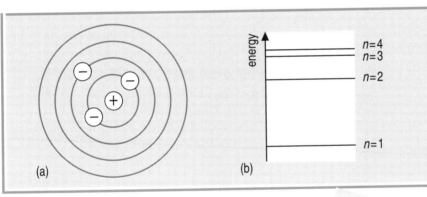

Figure 3.13 (a) A pictorial representation of Bohr's model of the atom. (b) Bohr's model represented by a set of allowed electron energy levels

In Bohr's model of the atom, electrons could absorb energy and move to a more 'excited' state. They could then fall back to a state of lower energy, releasing energy as they fell. In this model, such energy transitions were possible between certain fixed energy levels. (Bohr pictured these levels as different orbits of electrons around the nucleus.)

Because the differences in energy between levels were exact (or 'discrete') amounts of energy, only certain energy transitions were allowed by this model. Energy

NIELS BOHR (1885–1962)

Niels Bohr was one of the century's greatest scholars of physics. He first made his name by formulating a quantum theory of the atom for which he was awarded the Nobel prize for physics in 1922. As quantum theory developed, he became one of its leading exponents. Later in his life, he did extremely important work on nuclear physics.

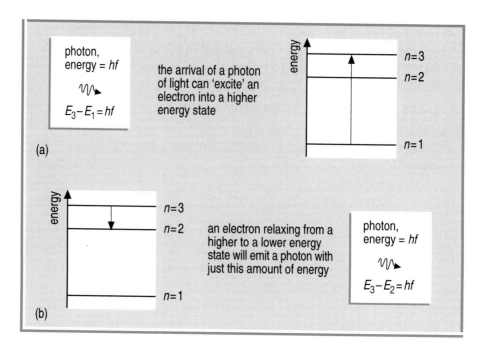

Figure 3.14
Electron transitions between energy levels

could therefore be absorbed or emitted only in packets or quanta. This was the link in Bohr's atomic model to quantum theory. The mechanism was as follows: the missing wavelengths in an absorption spectrum would correspond to photons of light having been absorbed, photons with exactly the same energy as required for a transition between energy levels, as shown in Figure 3.14(a). An emission spectrum, on the other hand, revealed only those photons of light emerging as a result of transitions from high to low energy levels as shown in Figure 3.14(b).

Most electrons would exist naturally in their lowest energy state, the ground state, labelled, $n = 1$ in Figure 3.14. The line spectrum of hydrogen gas as observed by Balmer represented a set of transitions to the second energy level, $n = 2$. The complete energy level diagram for an isolated electron of a hydrogen atom is shown in Figure 3.15. Notice how the levels bunch together as they approach an upper limit. The transitions shown by arrows from the higher energy levels down to $n = 2$ for hydrogen is known as the Balmer series.

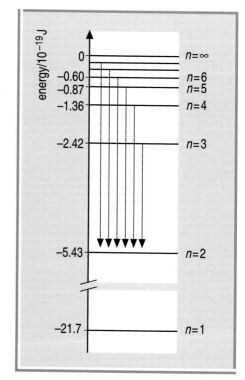

Figure 3.15 An energy level diagram for hydrogen

Using the values for the energy of each energy level given in Figure 3.15, work out the energy and frequency of a photon emitted as an electron as it makes the transition between levels $n = 5$ and $n = 1$. Would an emitted photon from such a transition have greater or lower energy compared with the visible light that Balmer saw? ($h = 6.6 \times 10^{-34}$ J s.)

According to Figure 3.15

$$E_5 - E_1 = \left[(-0.87)-(-21.7)\right]\times 10^{-19} \text{ J}$$

$$= 20.8 \times 10^{-19} \text{ J}$$

Since

$$E_5 - E_1 = hf$$

then

$$f = \frac{E_5 - E_1}{h}$$

$$= \frac{20.8 \times 10^{-19} \text{ J}}{6.6 \times 10^{-34} \text{ J s}}$$

$$= 3.2 \times 10^{15} \text{ Hz (to two significant figures)}$$

This frequency is greater than the frequency of visible light and so would correspond to a photon beyond the blue end of the spectrum, an ultraviolet photon, which would not be visible to the naked eye and would have a greater energy than a photon from the visible region.

No wonder it took another few years before the ultraviolet spectrum of hydrogen was seen by another physicist, Theodore Lymann, who was director of the physics laboratory at Harvard University, USA (see Figure 3.16).

The complete hydrogen spectrum includes wavelengths corresponding to the transitions down to levels $n = 3$ and to $n = 4$, etc. These are small energy transitions and represent radiation in the infrared part of the spectrum. These were not seen until much later.

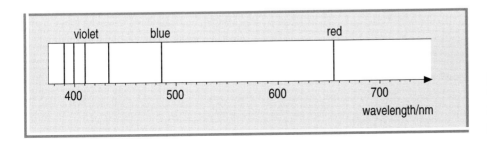

Figure 3.16
The main spectral lines in the Balmer series for hydrogen

Spectral lines and motion in space

In 1842, amidst the new discoveries in spectroscopy, the physicists Christian Doppler and Hippolyte Fizeau suggested that the motion of stars might be detected by looking for subtle changes in their line spectra. They knew that as objects moved away the light they emitted would be shifted towards the red end of the spectrum, i.e. the wavelengths of the light would increase a little. This is known as **red shift**. For stars moving towards the observer, the lines would move a little to the blue end of the spectrum, called blue shift. This effect is known as the **Doppler effect** (see Figures 3.17 and 3.18).

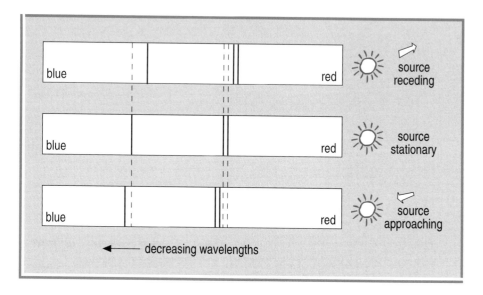

Figure 3.17
The Doppler effect in the spectra of stars

An important measurement to make when determining red and blue shifts is the fractional change in wavelength of any key spectral line. This fractional change in wavelength, $\dfrac{\Delta\lambda}{\lambda}$ can be related to the velocity, v, by

$$\frac{\Delta\lambda}{\lambda} \approx \frac{v}{c}$$

where c is the speed of light through space, approximately 3.0×10^8 m s^{-1}.

The Doppler effect has been a very useful tool in helping astronomers and cosmologists understand the Universe.

The example in Figure 3.18(c) has a particular significance to cosmologists who are interested in the origins of the Universe. It was the astronomer Edwin Hubble, using the Mount Wilson telescope during the period 1916 to 1917, who discovered that every galaxy displayed a spectral shift and in most cases this was a red shift. In addition, Hubble also found that the more distant galaxies were moving away faster. This startling discovery led cosmologists to suggest that we live in an expanding universe.

RELATION BETWEEN RED-SHIFT AND DISTANCE
FOR EXTRAGALACTIC NEBULAE

CLUSTER NEBULA IN	DISTANCE IN LIGHT-YEARS	RED-SHIFTS

VIRGO — 7,500,000 — H+K — 750 MILES PER SECOND

URSA MAJOR — 100,000,000 — 9,300 MILES PER SECOND

CORONA BOREALIS — 130,000,000 — 13,400 MILES PER SECOND

BOOTES — 230,000,000 — 24,400 MILES PER SECOND

HYDRA — 350,000,000 — 38,000 MILES PER SECOND

Red-shifts are expressed as velocities, c $d\lambda/\lambda$.
Arrows indicate shift for calcium lines H and K.
One light-year equals about 6 trillion miles,
or 6×10^{12} miles

Absorption spectrum showing red shift

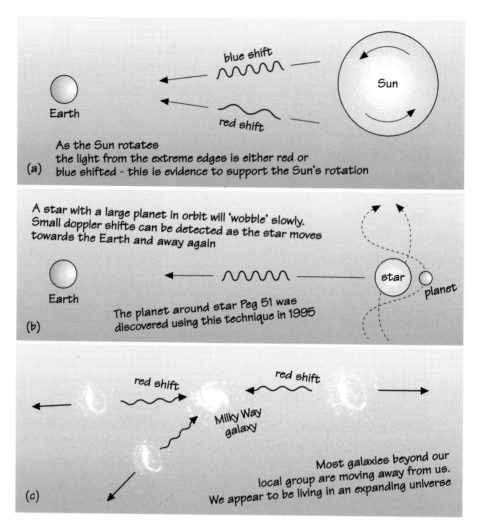

Figure 3.18
Some ways in which the Doppler effect is used in astronomy and cosmology

Q8 The 505 nm spectral line has been observed in a galaxy in the constellation of Bootes to be shifted to 565 nm. How fast is this galaxy moving and is it approaching or receding? ◆

 If all galaxies are moving away from us does this mean that we are in a special position at the centre of the Universe?

No, in an expanding universe any single vantage point will show all other galaxies moving away. The expansion will be seen by all observers.

Of course, cosmologists look both back and forward in time. If the Universe is currently expanding then two key questions arise: 'What are we expanding from?' and 'What will the Universe do eventually?'

Looking back in time

Was there a beginning, a point in time when it all started? What was there in the beginning? This is the event referred to as the **Big Bang**.

The actual age of the Universe as extrapolated from the present expansion rate is subject to great debate. Hubble calculated the expansion rate of the Universe but there is evidence today that the Hubble rate of expansion needs revising; however, a definitive value has yet to be agreed upon.

Is there any supporting evidence that there was in fact a Big Bang? George Gamow, a Russian-born physicist, predicted that the 'echo' of the Big Bang ought to be detectable from all directions in the form of low energy microwave radiation, corresponding to that emitted from a black body at a cool 2.7 K. In 1965, Arno Penzias and Robert Wilson, working with a radio telescope in New Jersey, USA, detected just such a background signal. **Microwave background** radiation, the echo of the Big Bang, did exist. This was perhaps the most convincing support possible for the Big Bang theory.

 2.7 K is about −270°C. How can such a cold object be considered to be radiating energy? Don't only warm objects radiate?

Yes, this is true. But 2.7 K is 2.7 degrees warmer than absolute zero!

 If the whole Universe is glowing with microwave radiation it should be possible to apply Wien's law to find a value for the wavelength at which most of this energy is radiated. Show that this wavelength, using Wien's displacement law given earlier and the fact that the temperature associated with the radiation is 2.7 K, is in the microwave region. (Microwaves occupy the mm to cm wavelength range of the electromagnetic spectrum.)

$$\lambda_{max} = \frac{2.9 \times 10^{-3}\,\mathrm{m\,K}}{2.7\,\mathrm{K}}$$

$$= 1.1 \times 10^{-3}\,\mathrm{m}\ \text{(to two significant figures)}$$

This wavelength is within the microwave range.

Recent measurements by the Cosmic Background Explorer satellite (CoBE), in 1992 found that there is a small ripple structure within the microwave background field. The background radiation is not perfectly uniformly distributed. Such a result has been welcomed by physicists as it allows a model to be proposed of local concentrations of matter that formed into clusters of galaxies.

Looking ahead in time

Will gravitational forces slow the expansion down or even reverse it? Do we live in a one-time 'open' universe with just the single expansion moving outwards forever? Or is there a possibility of a reversal of the expansion to produce a 'closed' Universe, the so-called Big Crunch?

On the question of whether there is enough matter in the Universe to slow down and eventually reverse the expansion, current estimates show that there doesn't appear to be enough matter. However, there may be mass out in space that is not yet accounted for. It may be invisible or unseeable. The search for such 'dark matter', including black holes, is a live issue in modern astrophysics.

Alternative models include the possibility that the Universe may be oscillating. If the laws of physics break down under an intense gravitational collapse then perhaps repulsive forces could come into play to repeat the original expansion. A feature of such a model is that there is no requirement for a starting-point. Time can be considered as never starting and never ending; no Big Bang, no Big Crunch just one harmonious cosmic pendulum.

3.5 Public science – cosmic background radiation

CoBE was launched in 1989 by the American space agency NASA. Its purpose was to probe the cosmic microwave background radiation, the faint glow that permeates the whole of space left over from the tremendous heat of the Big Bang. When CoBE's scientists had analysed some of the information from the satellite they claimed that their data showed ripples in the background radiation that were the first traces of the structures of galaxies and galaxy clusters that we now see.

Photograph from CoBE showing variations in temperature of cosmic background radiation

All over the world, CoBE was front-page news. The importance of CoBE was such that not only did the British quality broadsheets – the *Guardian*, the *Independent*, the *Telegraph* and *The Times* – give whole pages over to the story, but it made the tabloids, such as the *Sun*, as well. Here are two articles, one from the *Sun*, 'We find secret of the creation', and one from the *Independent*, 'How the universe began'.

Read the two articles and then answer Questions 9 and 10.

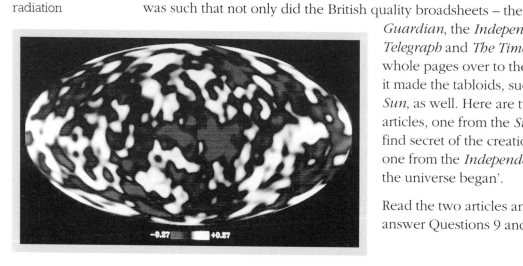

WE FIND SECRET OF THE CREATION

AND IT ONLY TOOK 15 BILLION YEARS

AMERICAN scientists using a satellite dubbed the Time Machine believe they have discovered the secret of how the universe was formed.

The NASA space probe orbiting the Earth has picked up radiation which has taken 15 billion years to arrive from the edge of the cosmos travelling at the speed of light.

It is energy given off by massive ripples of matter created after the universe's rapid expansion following the Big Bang. Using the satellite's radiation readings, scientists have created an amazing picture of the universe just after it was created. The ripples of matter are shown as patchy areas in our picture. The force of gravity made the ripples clump together, creating the stars, galaxies and clusters of galaxies.

NASA's Cosmic Background Explorer's discovery is the highpoint of a 28-year quest to solve one of science's most puzzling riddles.

Whispy

California University astrophysicist George Smooth said: "We have found evidence for the birth of the universe."

He added the ripples, which look like wispy clouds, were "the largest and most ancient structures in the universe."

Invisible to the naked eye, they were 59 billion trillion miles long. The radiation the ripples gave off has travelled at 186,000 miles a second, reaching Earth 15 billion years later.

The satellite has made more than 300 million measurements since its 1989 launch. Finding the radiation has helped build a picture of the young universe and led to the NASA probe being dubbed "a wonderful time machine".

TV astronomer Heather Couper said: "It's a bit like mixing a cake.

The big bang was the spoon, which causes lumps in the mixture.

"Those lumps were the seeds of the universe. Over millions of years they got bigger and bigger, until they formed stars and galaxies."

Prize

Michael Turner, a University of Chicago physicist, said: "The significance of this discovery cannot he overstated.

"They have found the Holy Grail cosmology.

"If it is correct, this certainly would have to be considered for the Nobel Prize."

Chief NASA scientist John Mather said: "Our discovery reveals for the first time the primeval seeds that developed into the modern universe.

"It tells us how the universe developed from an almost featureless explosion into something that's been broken up into clusters of galaxies and huge empty spaces."

Dr Alan Heavens an expert in the formation of galaxies added: "This is like discovering a fantastic treasure.

"We all knew these seeds should be out there and we have found them."

Evidence collected by the satellite also supports the theory that up to 90 per cent of the universe is made of invisible "dark matter" that scientists haven't been able to identify.

Light

The first decisive evidence supporting the Big Bang theory came in 1964 when scientists detected its "afterglow".

Until the latest breakthrough, the biggest-known structure in the universe was the "great wall" – an arc of galaxies about 200 million light years long.

(*Sun* 24 April 1992)

A Nasa spacecraft has detected echoes of the galaxies' birth fourteen thousand million years ago. The discovery about the formation of the universe after the Big Bang has been hailed by excited scientists as the Holy Grail of cosmology. **Susan Watts** and **Tom Wilkie** report.

How the universe began

FOURTEEN thousand million years ago the universe hiccuped. Yesterday, American scientists announced that they have heard the echo.

A Nasa spacecraft has detected ripples at the edge of the Cosmos which are the fossilised imprint of the birth of the stars and galaxies around us today.

According to Michael Rowan-Robinson, a leading British cosmologist, "What we are seeing here is the moment when the structures we are part of – the stars and galaxies of the universe – first began to form."

The ripples were spotted by the Cosmic Background Explorer (Cobe) satellite and presented to excited astronomers at a meeting of the American Physical Society in Washington yesterday.

"Oh wow … you can have no idea how exciting this is," Carlos Frenk, an astronomer at Durham University, said yesterday. "All the world's cosmologists are on the telephone to each other at the moment trying to

work out what these numbers mean."

Cobe has provided the answer to a question that has baffled scientists for the past three decades in their attempts to understand the structure of the Cosmos. In the 1960s two American researchers found definitive evidence that a Big Bang had started the whole thing off about 15 billion years ago. But the Big Bang would have spread matter like thin gruel evenly throughout the universe. The problem was to work out how the lumps (stars, planets and galaxies) got into the porridge.

"What we have found is evidence for the birth of the universe," said Dr George Smoot, an astrophysicist at the University of California, Berkeley, and the leader of the Cobe team.

Dr Smoot and colleagues at Berkeley joined researchers from several American research organisations to form the Cobe team. These included the Goddard Space Flight Center, Nasa's Jet Propulsion laboratory, the Massachusetts Institute of Technology and Princeton University. Joel

Primack, a physicist at the University of California at Santa Cruz, said that if the research is confirmed, "it's one of the major discoveries of the century. In fact, it's one of the major discoveries of science."

Michael Turner, a University of Chicago physicist, called the discovery "unbelievably important". "The significance of this cannot be overstated. They have found the Holy Grail of cosmology … if it is indeed correct, this certainly would have to be considered for a Nobel Prize."

Since the ripples were created almost 15 billion years ago, their radiation has been travelling toward Earth at the speed of light. By detecting the radiation, Cobe is "a wonderful time machine" able to view the young universe, Dr Smoot said,

A remnant glow from the Big Bang is still around today, in the form of microwave radiation that has bathed the universe for the billions of years since the explosion. Galaxies must have formed by growing gravitational

Q9 List the number of scientific or technical pieces of information carried in each story. How much 'general education' about cosmology did each of the papers feel it needed to give its readers?

(*Hint:* Try to list the things you would learn about CoBE itself and what it has discovered about the Cosmic Microwave Background Radiation, in particular, and separately list information about cosmology in general. You might expect the *Independent* article to be very informative. But you may be surprised at just how much the *Sun* also had for its readers, albeit in a much more condensed form.) ◆

Q10 In the days that followed, several papers dealt with the significance of CoBE for religion. Why do you think this was? ◆

forces bringing matter together. To produce a "lumpy" universe, radiation from the Big Bang should itself show signs of being lumpy.

Cobe, which has been orbiting 500 miles above the Earth since the end of 1989, has instruments on board which are sensitive to this extremely old radiation. The ripples Cobe has found are the first hard evidence of the long-sought lumpiness in the radiation.

Cobe detected almost imperceptible variations in the temperature of the radiation, which measures 270C below zero. Those variations – only about thirty-millionths of a degree – represent slight differences in the density of matter at the edge of the universe, ripples of wispy clouds surrounded by slightly less dense matter, the scientists said yesterday. The smallest ripples the satellite picked up stretch across 500 million light years of space.

Cobe has taken a snapshot of the universe just 300,000 years after Big Bang itself – at a point in time when the foggy fireball of radiation and matter produced by the explosion cooled down. "The results also show that the idea of a Big Bang model is once again brilliantly successful," Professor Rowan-Robinson, of London University, said.

He described the ripples as similar to the chaotic pattern of waves you might see from an aeroplane window flying over an ocean. "I can be pretty confident now that if we had an even bigger telescope in space we could see the fluctuations that are the early signs of individual galaxies themselves. It's just a matter of technology now," he added.

The point in time of Cobe's snapshot is known as "the epoch of recombination". At this point, the early galaxies began to form and light from these galaxies, released from the foggy soup of radiation, was set free to be picked up by modern astronomers with their telescopes.

"Further analysis of Cobe's results will shed light on the identity of the mysterious dark matter that we know contributes most of the mass of the universe," Dr Carlos Frenk, of Durham University, said yesterday. This mystery dark matter is scientists' best guess at explaining why the universe is lumpy.

Astronomers have worked out that there ought to be far more matter around for today's galaxies to have formed than they have observed. One of the leading theories to get round this is the Dark Matter theory, which says that about 99 per cent of the matter of the universe is invisible to us. This theory predicts fluctuations in the background radiation of exactly the size Cobe has observed. "Because these had not been seen, the theoreticians were beginning to get worried that they had got it wrong," Professor Rowan-Robinson said.

"If Cobe had found no ripples the theoreticians would have been in disarray; their best shot at understanding how galaxies were formed would have been disproved," he added. "The cold dark matter theory is a very beautiful one which makes very exact predictions about what the size of these fluctuations should be. How big they are depends on how fast they are able to grow. These results are just the size that the theory predicts."

However, Arnold Wolfendale, the Astronomer Royal, sounded a note of caution. "We don't want another cold fusion," he said. The scientific community must examine the results before shouting too loudly about their importance. "There is no doubt that, if verified, this is a very important result. Detecting these small fluctuations is very difficult. Another group reported having picked up similar fluctuations last year, then later found they were due to cosmic rays. At the frequencies our colleagues in the US are working at, cosmic rays should not be a problem, but there is dust between the stars which can also produce radiation and make you think it is cosmological."

Martin Rees, Professor of Astrophysics at Cambridge University, said: "We needed equipment sensitive enough to pick up these fluctuations. We can expect in the next year or so there will be other observations from the ground corroborating this."

He said the results opened up a whole new area of astronomy. "Now we have seen them we can start analysing them. We can learn a lot about the history of the universe – what happened when. We might find, for example, that there was a second foggy era after the original fog lifted."

(*Independent,* 24 April 1992)

Carlos Frenk is a cosmologist. Currently, he holds the Chair of Astrophysics at the University of Durham, where he studies the large-scale properties of the Cosmos. A few years ago, he was part of a team that discovered that the Universe was structured on much larger scales than anyone had previously realized, raising the question of just how such structures formed from the smooth Big Bang. Frenk's most recent work has been to use a massive computer to simulate how the galaxies and clusters of galaxies we see today could have formed from the ripples detected by the CoBE satellite during the 15 billion years for which the Universe has been evolving.

We interviewed Professor Frenk about his interest in cosmology and his work with the CoBE satellite.

Carlos Frenk

Interview with Professor Carlos Frenk

To many young people thinking about their future and what career they might follow, the idea of studying cosmology is an awesome prospect. It seems at the same time very abstract and extremely complicated. What motivated you to follow this path?

If you take a lot of astronomers, they always wanted to study astronomy right from when they were kids. That wasn't so with me. When I was at school in Mexico I actually wanted to be a physicist. But then I came to Cambridge in the late 1970s and I wanted to study some fundamental aspect of physics. So I looked around with the help of my professors. I looked at work on Einstein's general relativity, but I felt that had taken us as far as it could at the time. I considered particle physics, but that seemed to be moving rather slowly.

It was in cosmology where it seemed to me most of the exciting problems remained. There was the problem of how to form galaxies out of the smooth Big Bang and how we could measure and understand the exact nature of the cosmic microwave background radiation. I felt it was cosmology that was the really exciting area and I made my decision to go into this field over the period of about a week. Luckily for me, I made the right decision.

As to cosmology being complicated, I do not think it is more difficult than other areas of physics. That's true of a lot of astronomy. If you take Newton's mechanics, it is actually easier to apply them, say, to the planets in our solar system than to objects here on Earth because you do not have to worry about complicating factors such as friction.

In order to make progress in cosmology we simply make a fundamental assumption that the Universe as a whole works according to the laws of physics. That is a very important assumption known as the **Copernican principle**. Put differently, the Copernican principle states that we do not occupy a special privileged position. The Universe must look the same to every other observer wherever they are and so the same laws of physics work everywhere.

People think that cosmology is difficult because it deals with the whole Universe and that makes it difficult because the Universe is very big. Well, size isn't everything, and by using the Copernican principle we introduce an underlying simplicity into the field.

But isn't that an enormous leap of faith? How can you be sure that physics does work the same way everywhere in the Universe?

The question you ask is: 'Are the laws of physics that we derive in the laboratory applicable to the Universe as a whole?' OK, we take that as a starting assumption and then we look to see if there are any violations. Are there any violations in the way stars evolve? Did the laws work right the way back to the Big Bang? Well, the Copernican principle is a fundamental assumption, but without it you could not even get started.

But you can also see what sort of predictions you end up with if you do make this assumption. For instance, if you apply the laws of gravity to large scales you find that you need something we call dark matter, matter that you cannot see by ordinary methods. This dark matter is necessary to hold galaxies together as they spin round and to control the movement of stars within galaxies.

Now we have not found this dark matter yet and there are some people who believe that there is no such thing. They propose to ditch the Copernican principle and assume instead that the laws of gravity change to explain how galaxies hang together. But attempts to work out a new law of gravity have failed. The predictions the theory made were not verified and it proved impossible to generalize the theory. That meant that changing the laws of gravity leads you to a situation where you just cannot have any cosmology at all.

Similarly, people proposed changing the laws of physics when quasars were first found. These are objects which appear to be as bright as stars, but are really very, very distant. To be that bright they must be incredibly energetic and conditions in quasars must be really extreme. But you could learn nothing about them by proposing that the laws of physics changed. Instead, it is by assuming that the laws stay the same that you find these new phenomena tell us something really interesting. So the Copernican principle is a 'leap of faith', but it's a working 'leap of faith'.

When the story broke in April 1992 that the CoBE satellite had detected ripples in the cosmic microwave background radiation dating from just 300 000 years after the Big Bang, the media really blew up the story to give it front page coverage. Do you think CoBE was that significant? Or do you think this was a case of 'media hype'?

My view is that, in this case, the media were extremely impressive. They got their facts right and they appreciated the significance of the story. Now you always have to make a few allowances for the media and I like to distinguish between what the quality press and the tabloids are saying but they, by and large, did a magnificent job with CoBE.

CoBE's results were highly significant for two reasons. Firstly, what the satellite discovered was the fossil record of galaxies. To make an analogy, CoBE found the 'missing link' between the simple, smooth early Universe and the complicated structured one we have today. Secondly, unlike other sciences, cosmology only makes a few predictions which you test. If you take the physics of atoms and electrons, that makes lots of predictions, then, there are lots of atoms and electrons. But there is only one Universe. One of the predictions cosmology did make, however, was that there should be ripples in the cosmic microwave background radiation and CoBE found them.

It was highly significant that CoBE did find them. This is an area in which there is a connection between quantum mechanics, which deals with the world on a very small scale, and the large-scale Universe. Connecting these two regions together through the ripples was very important.

Clearly cosmologists have made great progress over the last few years in understanding the Universe all the way back to the Big Bang. Is everything now settled or do you think that young scientists, coming into the area in ten or fifteen years, will find the exciting challenges that attracted you?

In 2004, the European Space Agency will launch a satellite called Cobra-Samba, which will do the same job as CoBE but in much greater detail. That will be very exciting. Cobra-Samba will look at the cosmic microwave background radiation at much higher **spatial resolution** than CoBE, which will enable us to see the details of the structure of the early Universe rather than just saying that it does have structure. And then I think cosmology will tend to split into two areas.

For the first area, there are three or four fundamental constants – the Hubble constant, which tells us how fast the Universe is expanding, the cosmological constant, and the density and composition of the Universe – which really control our model of the cosmos. At present we do not know the values of these constants anything like precisely enough, and our models have too much freedom. I think this is an area which will be being addressed then in the next decade so that in ten to fifteen years cosmology will have become a really quantitative science like other branches of physics.

For the second area, we want to know in detail how the galaxies we see today, spirals, ellipticals and so on, really formed from the early Universe. That will draw attention to the fundamental physics underlying galaxies, including the question of the composition of dark matter and the nature of the Universe prior to what we call the Planck Time, an incredibly short 10^{-43} seconds after the Big Bang.

I am very optimistic that we will be solving some very big questions in cosmology in the next ten to fifteen years as a result of new and better data from Cobra-Samba and other advances. But there may also be some very big surprises in store. With something as big as the Universe, you can never be sure. After all, you are asking the biggest questions that can be asked.

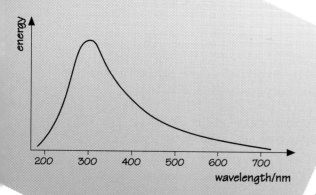

Figure 3.19
Black-body radiation

Q11 Carlos Frenk makes a distinction between the broadsheet and tabloid coverage of CoBE. Look back to the two newspaper articles. To what extent do you think he was justified in making this distinction? ◆

Q12 Figure 3.19 shows how the energy of radiation emerging from a black body is distributed among different wavelengths.

(a) Explain what is meant by the term 'black body'?

(b) (i) At which wavelength does this body emit most energy? (ii) Use this information and Wien's law to estimate the temperature of this body.

(c) On a copy of the Figure 3.19, show what you would expect to happen to the distribution if the black body were allowed to cool to half the present temperature. Indicate any significant differences between the two graphs.

(d) Show the spectrum of a third body, which was found to emit light at only three wavelengths: 300 nm, 400 nm and 700 nm.

(e) Explain how these three wavelengths might be related to the structure of energy levels in atom. ◆

Q13 (a) Describe what is meant by the following terms: (i) photon, (ii) photoelectron, (iii) work function.

(b) A 24 W lamp emits light of wavelength 5.0×10^{-7} m. Calculate (i) the frequency of the radiation emitted, (ii) the energy within each photon, (iii) the number of photons emitted each second.

(c) What would happen to your answers if the same lamp were run on only half power?

(d) In a demonstration of the photoelectric effect a student used light of wavelength 220 nm. She found that the photoelectrons could be captured by a metal plate provided it had a potential of at least −4.5 V.

Explain what would happen to the photoelectrons if the potential of the plate were (i) 0.5 V, (ii) −6.0 V, (iii) +6.0 V.

(e) Use the information in part (d) to calculate a value for the work function of the metal used. ◆

Q14 Figure 3.20 shows an absorption spectrum obtained from a distant nebula.

(a) Explain how a distant nebula can be responsible for producing an absorption spectrum.

(b) Why are the missing lines only at certain wavelengths?

(c) How can a spectrum such as this tell scientists about: (i) the gases present in the nebula, (ii) the movement of the gas cloud responsible for the nebula.

(d) Figure 3.21 presents three proposed models to show the energy levels of atoms responsible for the absorption spectrum. Which one best fits the spectral evidence? Explain why. ◆

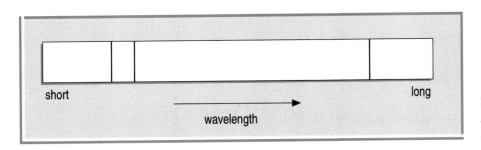

Figure 3.20
An absorption spectrum

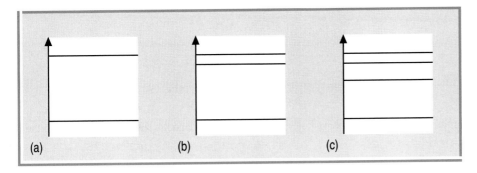

Figure 3.21
Three energy level models

Q15 (a) Outline one piece of evidence to suggest that light is: (i) a wave, (ii) a particle.

(b) The following are phenomena that can be explained using a model of light. For each one state which model best explains the observations and then offer an explanation using your chosen model: (i) the photoelectric effect, (ii) Young's interference fringes, (iii) reflection at a plane mirror. ◆

Achievements

After working through this section you should be able to:

- explain what is meant by a 'black body' and relate the energy from a star to that of a black body

- outline the stages in the life cycle of a star

- appreciate the part played by 'quantum theory' in understanding the photoelectric effect

- interpret spectral lines in terms of quanta and atomic energy levels

- use the relationships between speeds, energies and wavelengths to calculate the speed of a galaxy, photoelectron energies and photon energies

- appreciate how spectral lines yield information about stars, their composition and motion

- explain how spectral lines have helped to indicate that the Universe is expanding.

Glossary

Absorption spectrum A pattern of spectral colours (lines) missing from the spectrum. The wavelengths of these lines provide a precise key to the identification of elements responsible for the spectrum. See also *Emission spectrum.*

Amplitude modulation The addition of information to a radio wave (or other 'carrier') as a fluctuation in its amplitude.

Angular momentum The 'moment of momentum'. A measure of the momentum possessed by a spinning object. Spinning objects require a turning force to stop and start them spinning.

Big Bang The point at the start of time when the complete Universe came into being in a massive explosion of energy.

Black body An object that emits a characteristic broad spread of radiation, the distribution of wavelengths depending on its temperature.

Black hole A point of immense mass in space with enormous gravitational attraction such that even light cannot escape.

Copernican principle The principle that states that the Universe looks the same to every observer wherever they are and so the laws of physics work everywhere. In other words, Earth does not occupy a privileged position at the centre of the Universe as the Greeks thought.

Cosmic singularity An event in space that marks the start or end of a process and the exact understanding of what happens beyond the event is unclear.

Diffraction The spreading out of wave energy from holes or around obstacles that get in the path of the waves

Dispersion The separation of colours of light due to refraction, as with a prism.

Doppler effect The observed change in frequency of radiation when there is motion between the observer and the source of the radiation.

Emission spectrum A pattern of spectral colours (lines) present in the spectrum. The wavelengths of these lines provide a precise key to the identification of elements responsible for the spectrum. See also *Absorption spectrum*

Event horizon The point beyond which no radiation can escape. It marks the outer edge of a black hole – the point of no return.

Frequency modulation The addition of information to a radio wave (or other 'carrier') as a fluctuation in its frequency. (The SLIPP unit *Physics Phones Home* has more information on modulation.)

Microwave background The cool electromagnetic waves that come from all parts of space and are thought to represent what remains of the radiation from the Big Bang.

Neutron star A collapsed star, which at the end of its life has enough gravitational effect in its dense core to compress its atoms so that nuclei are forced together.

Photoelectric effect The ejection of electrons from a metal when light above a threshold frequency is shone on to the surface of the metal.

Photoelectrons Electrons knocked out of a metal by bombardment with high energy photons.

Pulsar A spinning neutron star that emits a jet of radio waves as it spins.

Quantum A small discrete lump of energy.

Red giant A dying star that has exploded in the final phases of its life, forcing cool hydrogen outwards.

Red shift The effect that occurs when a star moves away from an observer and the spectral lines from the star appear at fractionally longer wavelengths. See also *Doppler effect*.

Refraction The change of speed that occurs when a wave moves from one medium to another. This will cause light to bend as it enters glass from air, for example.

Spatial resolution The smallest angular separation at which two objects can be distinguished by an observer as separate.

Threshold frequency The frequency of light below which no photoelectrons will be emitted from a metal. Each photon of light having less energy than the work function of the metal. See *work function*.

Wave–particle duality The flexible approach to waves and particles taken by physicists. Particles can show wave-like properties and waves can behave like particles.

White dwarf A collapsed star with very high surface temperature towards the end of its life.

Work function The energy required to enable an electron to escape the surface attraction of a metal.

Answers to Ready to Study test

R1

Light from your hair is reflected by the mirror and some rays pass into your eye. You see an image of yourself behind the mirror. (See Figure 3.22.)

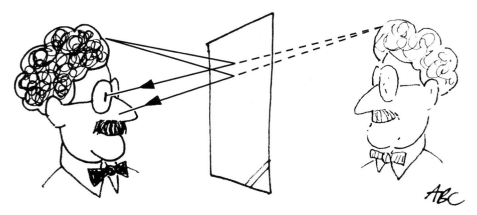

Figure 3.22 Answer to R1

R2

(a) The light is being refracted. Its speed reduces as it enters the prism and increases again as it leaves.

(b) The wavelength of the light decreases as it slows down. The frequency remains constant.

(c) When the speed changes so does the direction.

R3

(a) The correct order is: X-rays, ultraviolet rays, red light, radio waves

(b) You may have added any of the bold terms in the positions shown: **Gamma-rays**, X-rays, ultraviolet rays, **blue light**, red light, **infrared rays**, **microwaves**, radio waves.

R4

Both (a) and (b) will result in a wave like the one shown in Figure 3.23.

R5

(a)

(i)

$$p = mv$$

$$= 0.1\,\text{kg} \times 20\,\text{ms}^{-1}$$

$$= 2.0\,\text{kgms}^{-1}$$

(ii)

$$E_K = \frac{1}{2}mv^2$$

$$= 0.5 \times 0.1\,\text{kg} \times \left(20\,\text{ms}^{-1}\right)^2$$

$$= 20\,\text{J}$$

(b) If the velocity were doubled the momentum would double (the kinetic energy would increase four times as it depends on the square of the speed).

R6

The frog is in for a nasty surprise. Two waves will reach it, one from each side of the rock and they will be in phase as the difference in the length of the journey is two wavelengths. They will add to give the frog twice the displacement of a single wave: an effect known as constructive interference.

Answers to questions in the text

Q1

Using Wien's law

$$T = \frac{2.9 \times 10^{-3}\,\text{m K}}{240 \times 10^{-9}\,\text{m}}$$

$$= 1.2 \times 10^4\,\text{K (to two significant figures)}$$

Q2

(a) From Figure 3.3, $\lambda_{max} = 480\,\text{nm}$. This is a blue/green colour near the middle of the electromagnetic spectrum.

(b) Using Wien's law

$$T = \frac{2.9 \times 10^{-3}\,\text{m K}}{480 \times 10^{-9}\,\text{m}}$$

$$= 6.0 \times 10^3\,\text{K (to two significant figures)}$$

(c) If this were the temperature of a black body, the surface would appear white.

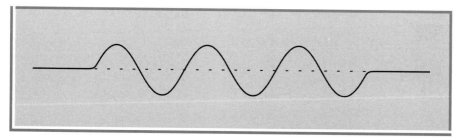

Figure 3.23
Answer to R4

Q3

There are seven possible sources of the pulses suggested by the article: white dwarf stars; neutron stars; double neutron star systems; very dense vibrating stars; supernovae explosions; a very faint red star; a very faint yellow star.

Q4

The theory that proposes that a vibrating white dwarf is the source of the pulses predicts a certain range of periods. The observed period of a quarter second must be at the extreme end of that range. If other pulsars were to be found with even shorter periods the theory would collapse. This is a problem because the equipment at that time was unable to detect shorter periods.

Q5

Maximum kinetic energy = stopping potential
$$\times \text{electron charge}$$
$$= -6.5\,\text{V} \times \left(-1.6 \times 10^{-19}\,\text{C}\right)$$
$$= 1.04 \times 10^{-18}\,\text{J}$$
$$= 1.0 \times 10^{-18}\,\text{J}$$
(to 2 significant figures)

Q6

The work function
$$\Phi = hf - E_{K\max}$$
$$= (6.6 \times 10^{-34}\,\text{J}\,\text{s} \times 0.88 \times 10^{16}\,\text{Hz})$$
$$- (1.04 \times 10^{-18}\,\text{J})$$
$$= 4.8 \times 10^{-18}\,\text{J} \text{ (to two significant figures)}$$

Q7

$$p = mv$$
$$= 1.7 \times 10^{-27}\,\text{kg} \times 1.2 \times 10^{8}\,\text{ms}^{-1}$$
$$= 2.04 \times 10^{-19}\,\text{kg}\,\text{ms}^{-1}$$

$$\lambda = \frac{h}{p}$$
$$= \frac{6.6 \times 10^{-34}\,\text{J}\,\text{m}}{2.04 \times 10^{-19}\,\text{kg}\,\text{ms}^{-1}}$$
$$= 3.2 \times 10^{-15}\,\text{m} \text{ (to two significant figures)}$$

Q8

The Doppler shift is to a longer wavelength and so the galaxy is receding. The speed of recession is found from

$$\frac{\Delta\lambda}{\lambda} = \frac{v}{c}$$
$$v = c\frac{\Delta\lambda}{\lambda}$$
$$= 3.0 \times 10^{8}\,\text{ms}^{-1}\frac{\left(565 - 505\right) \times 10^{-9}\,\text{m}}{505 \times 10^{-9}\,\text{m}}$$
$$= 3.0 \times 10^{8}\,\text{ms}^{-1}\frac{60 \times 10^{-9}\,\text{m}}{505 \times 10^{-9}\,\text{m}}$$
$$= \frac{180 \times 10^{8}\,\text{ms}^{-1}}{505}$$
$$= 3.56 \times 10^{7}\,\text{ms}^{-1}$$
$$= 3.6 \times 10^{7}\,\text{ms}^{-1}$$
(to two significant figures)

Q9

You could list the following, there may be more.

Information	Independent	Sun
Big Bang 15 billion years ago	✔	✔
Radiation travels at speed of light	✔	✔
Remnant microwave radiation from Big Bang	✔	✔
Temperature range of radiation	✔	
Light years	✔	
Fluctuations in background radiation	✔	
Cosmic rays	✔	
Cosmic dust	✔	
15 billion years to arrive		✔
Gravity causes formation of stars etc.	✔	✔
Discovery of largest and most ancient structures in the Universe		✔
Wisps 59 billion trillion miles long		✔
Universe began to form 14 thousand million years ago	✔	
Evidence for birth of Universe	✔	✔
Dark matter	✔	✔
Great wall		✔
CoBE orbiting since 1989	✔	✔
First evidence of lumpiness	✔	
Differences in density of matter at the edge of the Universe – ripples	✔	
Ripples stretch across 500 million light years	✔	
CoBE snapshot 300,000 years after the Big Bang (epoch of recombination)	✔	
Expanding Universe		✔

Q10

The scientists' claims that the evidence from CoBE provided explanations for how the Universe formed does not leave any room for the creation of the Universe based on religious beliefs. There was therefore much discussion to be had about the effect of the scientific evidence on religious beliefs.

Q11

There was a lot of science in both reports. So, in this instance, Carlos Frenk isn't justified in making a clear distinction between the broadsheet and tabloid reports. (The original report in the *Independent* – a broadsheet paper – also included an informative illustration, which we did not have the space to reproduce here, showing the evolution of the Universe from the Big Bang to the emergence of life on Earth.)

Q12

(a) An object that radiates energy, the energy being a result only of the temperature of the body.

(b) (i) Using Figure 3.19, most energy is emitted at about 300 nm

(ii)

$$T = \frac{2.9 \times 10^{-3}\,\mathrm{m\,K}}{300 \times 10^{-9}\,\mathrm{m}}$$

$$= 9.7 \times 10^3\,\mathrm{K}\ \text{(to two significant figures)}$$

(c) Your graph should look similar to Figure 3.24.

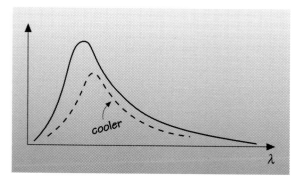

Figure 3.24 Answer to Question 12(c)

(d) The spectrum is shown in Figure 3.25.

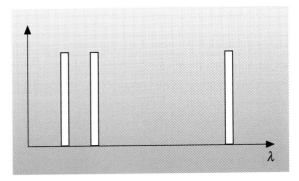

Figure 3.25 Answer to Question 12(d)

(e) The prescence of three wavelengths suggests that three energy transitions are possible. This can be achieved by a structure with a ground state energy and two higher levels of energy.

Q13

(a) (i) A particle of light radiation.

(ii) An electron knocked out of a metal by a photon.

(iii) The energy required for an electron to break free from a metal surface.

(b) (i)

$$f = \frac{c}{\lambda}$$

$$= \frac{3.0 \times 10^8 \, ms^{-1}}{5.0 \times 10^{-7} \, m}$$

$$= 6.0 \times 10^{14} \, Hz$$

(ii)

$$E = hf$$

$$= 6.6 \times 10^{-34} \, Js \times 6.0 \times 10^{14} \, Hz$$

$$= 4.0 \times 10^{-19} \, J \text{ (to two significant figures)}$$

(iii)

$$\frac{24 \, W}{4.0 \times 10^{-19} \, J} = 6.0 \times 10^{19} \, s^{-1}$$

(c) The frequency and energy answers would be the same, but at 12 W the number of photons per second would be half.

(d) (i) Electrons would be attracted to the plate.

(ii) No electrons would reach the plate – all would be repelled.

(iii) Electrons would be attracted to the plate.

(e)

$$qV = E_k$$

$$\quad = hf - \Phi$$

so

$$\Phi = hf - qV$$

$$= \frac{6.6 \times 10^{-34} \, Js \times 3.0 \times 10^8 \, ms^{-1}}{220 \times 10^{-9} \, m}$$

$$- \left(-1.6 \times 10^{-19} \, C \times \left(-4.5 \, V\right)\right)$$

$$= 1.8 \times 10^{-19} \, J$$

Q14

(a) A bright light source beyond the nebula will emit almost a continuous spectrum. The cooler nebula in front of the source will absorb some specific frequencies.

(b) Because the energy of the missing lines will match the exact energy differences inside an atom.

(c) (i) The gases present will convey their absorption spectral 'footprints'. These will be used to identify the gases.

(ii) The absorption lines may be seen to be Doppler shifted slightly. This will give us a clue to the dynamism of the nebula.

(d) Figure 3.21(b) fits best as within it there are three distinctly different energy transitions.

Q15

(a) (i) Interference fringes seen past Young's slits.

(ii) The photoelectric effect.

(b) (i) Particle model: the photons have to deliver their energy in a lump in order to interact with an electron.

(ii) Wave model: this depends on waves adding up and cancelling out – constructive and destructive interference.

(iii) Particle model: the laws of reflection are most simply demonstrated when using a particle model in which there are collisions similar to billiard ball collisions.

What is invisible, has been known about by everyone since before Galileo, but still remains a total mystery to science? Gravity of course. Yet gravitational forces are the very reason that stars form in the first place and that we can remain on a spinning planet to study them. To Isaac Newton, the gravitational forces between planets could easily be carried on invisible strings or spokes. He really didn't know. Today we think the forces might be carried by invisible particles called gravitons! It is amazing that with such uncertainty about what gravity actually is we can use equations to describe how it keeps Earth in orbit, how it can help to redirect space probes and how it produces black holes. One effect of gravity is to direct the path of solar system visitors such as comets. In this section we take a look at the story of the comet that recently crashed into Jupiter – comet Shoemaker–Levy 9. Gravity was responsible for its orbit around the Sun, for its disintegration into 26 fragments and for its eventual demise when it collided with Jupiter.

READY TO STUDY TEST

Before you begin this section you should be able to:

■ appreciate that Earth's gravity will pull a mass m towards the centre of Earth with a force, $F = mg$ and use this equation to determine weights

■ recall that on the surface the strength of Earth's gravity, g, is about 9.81 N kg^{-1} and use this value in calculations when appropriate

■ recall that a mass will accelerate at about 9.81 m s^{-2} when dropped near Earth's surface and use this value in calculations when appropriate

■ explain how the mass of an object is related to the number and type of particles within it

■ state why an unbalanced force is required to make an object accelerate

■ define density as density, $\rho = \dfrac{mass}{volume}$ and use this equation to calculate density

■ use Newton's three laws of motion.

QUESTIONS

R1 Sugar is often sold in 0.5 kg bags.

(a) What is the weight of a 0.5 kg bag of sugar.

(b) What is the mass of a 0.5 kg bag of sugar?

R2 Explain why a 0.5 kg packet of cornflakes takes up much more space in your shopping bag than the 0.5 kg bag of sugar.

R3 A 0.5 kg bag of sugar and a 0.5 kg box of cornflakes slip out of your shopping bag and fall to the ground. Describe the forces that act on each object on its way from the bag to the ground.

R4 A single cornflake dropped to the ground will accelerate as shown in Figure 4.1. Its velocity will increase to a greatest value, the terminal velocity.

(a) What will be the rate of change of velocity, i.e. the acceleration, of the cornflake just as it starts to fall?

(b) Before it hits the ground, the cornflake might be described as being in equilibrium. Explain why this might be said.

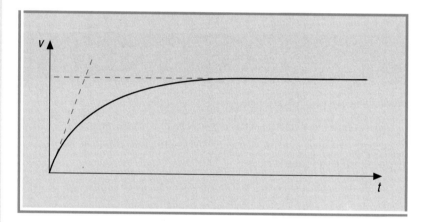

Figure 4.1
Velocity versus time graph

R5 Orbiting astronauts are often seen 'floating' about in their spacecraft. Can you explain why this happens? (This is a good discussion topic – try it with some friends.)

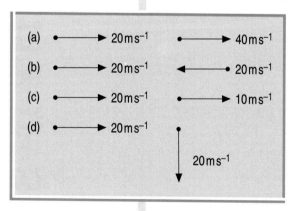

Figure 4.2
Moving objects

R6 Four moving objects are represented in Figure 4.2. The left-hand arrow shows each object's velocity at a particular moment in time and the right-hand arrow shows their velocity exactly 1 s later. For each object, say whether it is accelerating or not, and give a value if possible.

R7 A child is whirling a toy on a string in a circle around their head. What happens immediately after the string slips through the child's fingers? Why?

4.1 Moving in space

What is not held up will fall down

Most people have heard a story of the young Isaac Newton in his garden in Lincolnshire. Whether he saw an apple fall, and whether it hit him or whether it was just the thought that struck him, we'll never know. However, what is clear is that Newton at the time was puzzling over the forces that act on objects. Let's consider an apple on a tree in Lincolnshire. When hanging on the branch on a calm day the apple is motionless. We say it is in a 'state of **equilibrium**'. This means that all the forces on the apple will balance out, leaving no resultant force. Physicists represent forces on objects using a free body diagram.

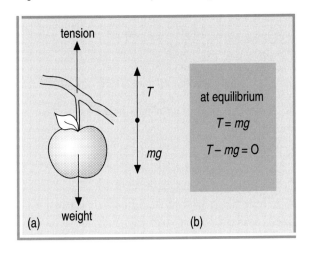

By adding the vertical forces acting on the apple we can show that there is no 'net' or unbalanced force. (See Figure 4.3.)

Figure 4.3
Forces acting on an apple

Forces have both magnitude and direction and so are **vector** quantities. This means they can be represented by arrows that show direction and size. The negative sign in Figure 4.3(b) indicates a force in an opposite direction. As it is in equilibrium the downward force, the apple's weight, is balanced by the upward pull of the branch.

When the time comes for the apple to fall, the upward force is removed (Figure 4.4). Only the downward force remains and this gravitational attraction pulls the apple towards Earth. The force acting on the apple is equal to its mass times its acceleration. The apple accelerates towards Earth at 9.81 m s^{-2} (often quoted as about 10 m s^{-2}). This value, 9.81 m s^{-2} or 9.81 N kg^{-1}, is known as 'g', the acceleration due to gravity. Gravity also pulls the Earth towards the apple but we don't notice the Earth moving.

Figure 4.4
A falling apple

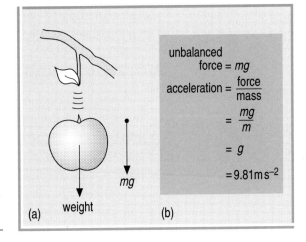

 Why don't we notice the Earth moving up towards the apple?

Earth's mass is so much larger than the apple's. Using $F = ma$, its acceleration can be shown to be about 1.7×10^{-24} m s^{-2}. No wonder we don't notice it!

Is the Earth attracted to the apple when the apple is held by the branch or is it an attraction that happens only when the apple falls? Try this out as a discussion topic with friends during a breaktime.

The value 9.81 N kg^{-1} is an average value. Earth is not completely spherical and so there are locations near the poles where the surface is closer to the centre and here 'g' is greater. At the Equator, where the spin of the Earth causes a bulge, 'g' is fractionally smaller. So if you want to lose weight visit the Equator!

Notice that there is a distinct difference between mass and weight. Mass is measured in kg but weight is a force in N. The weight of a mass, m, is easily calculated from weight = $m \times g$.

Q1 At the surface of the Moon the local gravity is about 1.6 N kg^{-1}.

(a) If a 0.5 kg bag of sugar were carried by a sweet-toothed cosmonaut on the Moon, what would it weigh?

(b) If it were dropped what would happen to its motion? ◆

A feature of the gravitational effect of Earth on our lives is the predictability of gravity. Everywhere we go on Earth gravity is there and, apart from local minor variations, g is the same strength everywhere. We describe this as a **uniform gravitational field**. 'Uniform' means the same size and direction wherever we go. Parallel lines can be used to show the vector nature of the **gravitational field** near Earth's surface. The direction of the field is the direction of the force on a free mass, e.g. an apple.

The strength of Jupiter's uniform gravitational field is about 24 N kg^{-1}. There is a uniform gravitational field at the surface of the Moon. Its strength is about 1.6 N kg^{-1}. It is interesting to note that the Moon's surface contains localized areas of denser rock, called mascons. These produce small local variations in surface gravity that are enough to cause NASA scientists to adjust the orbits of lunar probes.

Moving in a uniform field

Frictional forces dominate the movements we make every day. Because frictional forces cause us to waste energy, we strive to reduce friction, for example by oiling machinery. However, walking, cycling and travelling by bus would be impossible without friction with the road surface. To help us to simplify physics, let us consider a world without friction or with such low friction that we can ignore it. A smooth ice-skating rink will approximate to a frictionless world.

Moving horizontally poses no problem in such a perfect environment. Given an initial push a body will continue in a straight line until something stops it. No forces act in the direction of motion and no work is required to keep the motion going. This constant energy situation is possible with very smooth surfaces. We call such a surface a surface of **equipotential**. This means that a 1 kg mass at all places on the surface has the same potential energy. No work is needed to go from one place on the equipotential surface to another. However, to accelerate a mass along an equipotential surface is a different matter. This does involve an energy exchange and we will consider this next.

Moving satellites orbiting Earth move freely on an equipotential surface in space. Theirs is a friction-free world and one that is not very far from our Earth-bound ice-rink, shown in Figure 4.5. No work is required to keep a satellite in orbit, moving around an equipotential surface. (For satellites in space, the equipotential surface is an imaginary surface, not a real surface like an ice-rink.)

However, the problems of moving up or down in a gravitational field are well known to us. Climbing a hill or falling down a staircase are clearly energy transfer situations. The falling apple loses gravitational potential energy as it speeds up, gaining kinetic energy as a result. In a uniform field the energy transfers can be easily calculated from the work done when a force acts to move an object.

Work done = force × distance moved by the force

It is important to remember that the distance is not the distance moved by the object. Objects often keep moving long after the force has stopped. The work done is only for the duration that the force is applied.

When a rocket blasts off from a launch site the work done to lift a satellite is great indeed. Typically, to raise a satellite plus a rocket of total mass 4000 kg upwards by 1.00 m requires an amount of work to be done:

Figure 4.5
Skater and satellite moving along an equipotential surface

$$\text{work} = \text{force} \times \text{distance}$$

$$= mgh$$

$$= 4000\,\text{kg} \times 9.81\,\text{N}\,\text{kg}^{-1} \times 1.00\,\text{m}$$

$$= 39\,240\,\text{J}$$

$$= 3.92 \times 10^{4}\,\text{J or } 39\,200\,\text{J (to three significant figures)}$$

The work done to place this satellite at an orbiting height of about 800 km is therefore about 800 000 times this value, (the value of 'g' will be only marginally smaller at this height. 800 km is in fact quite close to Earth's surface.)

Of course, as the rocket rises its mass reduces because of the fuel it expends. This factor, together with the small reduction in 'g', needs to be taken into consideration by rocket scientists. The simple formula mgh is not sufficient for the real world of rocket launches.

Q2 Calculate the work done when (a) a 400 N force pushes a shopping trolley for a distance of 6.0 m, (b) a 0.50 kg bag of sugar is lifted 0.50 m from a shopping trolley to the checkout counter. ◆

Action and reaction

A rocket waiting for the countdown at the ESA Kourou launch site is in a state of equilibrium. The free body force diagram in Figure 4.6(a) shows how the weight is balanced by the reaction of the launchpad. For a rocket of mass 4000 kg, both these forces are calculated from

$$mg = 4000\,\text{kg} \times 9.81\,\text{m}\,\text{s}^{-2}$$

$$= 39\,240\,\text{N}$$

$$= 3.92 \times 10^{4}\,\text{N or } 39\,200\,\text{N (to three significant figures)}$$

Q3 Draw a free body force diagram of the launch mission manager, mass 80 kg, standing on the site. Draw a second diagram showing the forces when the manager jumps for joy at the sight of a successful lift-off. ◆

At lift-off the ignition causes an explosion of burning gases. The gas pressure in the reaction chamber acts in all directions. The exhaust leaving the bottom of the chamber results in the force at the top of the chamber being unbalanced. The engine, and hence the rocket, is pushed upwards. For as long as the explosive gases are forced out of the rocket engine there will be a reaction force on the rocket. (Unlike the launch mission manager, who only experienced his upthrust while his feet were on the ground.) Even when far away from the launchpad, the gases themselves being forced in one direction result in a reaction on the rocket to drive it forward. Isaac Newton recognized the importance of **action and reaction** forces in his third law of motion. However, the first

successful
space rocket
was launched
some 300 years
after his birth.

Satellites and
space probes use
this same action and
reaction principle to
change their orientation.
They don't need to carry
heavy fuel supplies as they
move along an equipotential
surface in orbit around Earth.
However, they do need to
reorientate themselves
occasionally, so they carry small
thruster motors and a gas supply. A
short blast of gas from a thruster
motor might provide a force of 100 N
that acts for about 5 s. A force acting for
a limited time results in an acceleration of
the vehicle and a change in momentum.

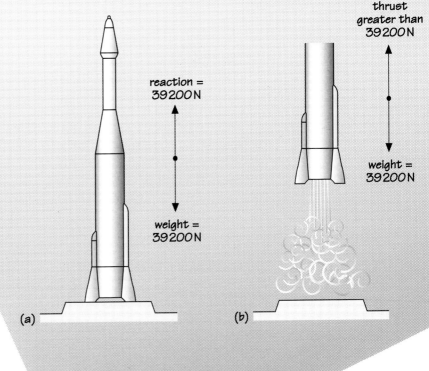

Figure 4.6
Rocket before and
after launch

$$\text{Force} = \text{mass} \times \text{acceleration}$$

$$= \text{mass} \times \frac{\text{change in velocity}}{\text{time}}$$

$$F = m \times \frac{(v - u)}{t}$$

$$F \times t = mv - mu \qquad\qquad (4.1)$$

Equation (4.1) shows that a force acting for a time will cause a change in
momentum of the vehicle. (Momentum is the product of mass and
velocity.)

so

$$\text{force} \times \text{time} = \text{change in momentum}$$

The product $F \times t$ is known as an **impulse** and its units are N s. The
change in momentum has units of kg m s^{-1}.

Q4 Show that the units of impulse, N s, are equivalent to the units of
momentum, kg m s^{-1}. ◆

Q5 (a) A space probe was subjected to a 4 s thrust of 150 N. Calculate
the impulse it received. (b) What effect did this have on the momentum
of the vehicle? ◆

Q6 The vehicle in Question 5 had a mass of 250 kg and was moving at 2000 m s^{-1}. The impulse was directed in the direction of the motion. How would this impulse change the velocity of the vehicle? ◆

When it is time for an orbiting satellite to be brought back to Earth, the satellite must be slowed down so that it falls towards Earth and enters Earth's atmosphere slowly. Changing the momentum of a satellite in space is a critical event. The Chinese spy satellite FSW1 went into unstable orbit following what is believed to have been a misfiring of its thrusters in 1993. It fell to Earth in March 1996, causing concern across Europe over where it would crash. Fortunately nobody was injured.

Let us look closely at the motion of a typical large satellite, mass 400 kg, in orbit at a speed of 7000 m s^{-1}. Let us assume that to fall to an Earth landing orbit the speed needs to be reduced to 6000 m s^{-1}. A 300 N thruster motor fired in the direction of motion is required to produce a 300 N force in the opposite direction for t seconds (see Figure 4.7).

$$\text{The desired change in momentum} = mv - mu$$

$$= m\left(7000\,\mathrm{m s}^{-1} - 6000\,\mathrm{m s}^{-1}\right)$$

$$= 400\,\mathrm{kg} \times 1000\,\mathrm{m s}^{-1}$$

$$= 4.00 \times 10^5\,\mathrm{N s}$$

This is to be provided by the impulse, $F \times t$, of the thruster motor, hence

$$F \times t = 4.00 \times 10^5\,\mathrm{N s}$$

therefore

$$t = \frac{4.00 \times 10^5\,\mathrm{N s}}{300\,\mathrm{N}}$$

$$= 1.333 \times 10^3\,\mathrm{s}$$

$$= 1.33 \times 10^3\,\mathrm{s} \text{ or } 1330\mathrm{s} \text{ (to three significant figures)}$$

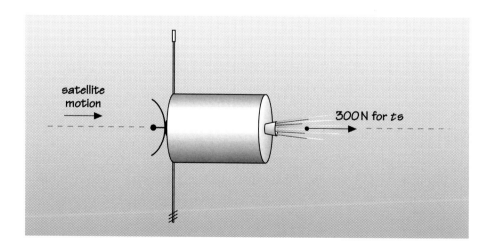

Figure 4.7
Satellite firing its thruster motor

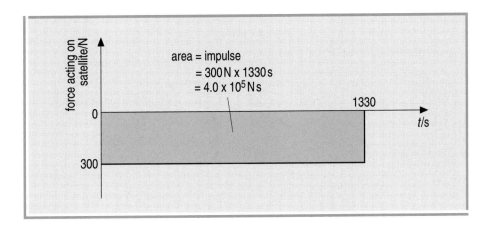

Figure 4.8
Force versus time graph for satellite

Q7 The graph shown in Figure 4.8 shows the force acting for a fixed time on the satellite.

(a) Sketch a graph to show how the acceleration of the satellite changed during this time and another.

(b) Sketch another graph to show how the velocity changed.

(c) What does the area under graph (a) represent? ◆

Spinning in space

There are times when a satellite needs to rotate through an angle. The Hubble Space Telescope needs to do this to look at different objects. Thrusters operate for short times to achieve this by producing a turning force or 'torque'. A turning impulse will produce an angular acceleration (the satellite will start to rotate). We say that the satellite has been given **angular momentum**. This means that it is a rotating mass that will require a reverse impulse to stop it spinning. Spinning ice skaters, spinning cricket balls and rotating planets all have angular momentum. (See Appendix 4.1 for further work on angular momentum.)

Once a rotational impulse is over, a satellite will continue to rotate at a constant rate until the reverse impulse stops it. Neil Armstrong's *Gemini V* flight was the first docking of a manned craft with an unmanned *Agena* target vehicle. Shortly after docking one of the thrusters jammed on. The force of this thruster would normally be balanced by a twin on the other side of the craft's centre of gravity. The failure produced a turning force that set the two craft spinning at about 1 revolution per minute. Armstrong corrected the spin and undocked, but so much fuel had been expended that the flight was cut short.

Figure 4.9(a) overleaf shows a satellite in equilibrium, and then in (b) under the action of a rotational force. In (c) the second force acts to reduce the spin to a new equilibrium in (d).

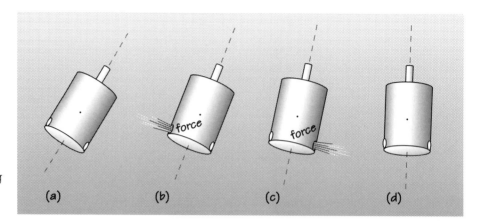

Figure 4.9
Thrusters producing a turning force on a space vehicle

(a)   (b)   (c)   (d)

Moving in circles

The entire Universe is composed of systems of bodies in orbit around other bodies. All are being forced in one direction or another by their mutual gravitational pull. The Moon and the Hubble Space Telescope orbit Earth, Earth orbits the Sun, the moons Phobos and Deimos orbit Mars, the Sun orbits the centre of the Milky Way galaxy, and so on. The motions are all elliptical but most elliptical orbits approximate to a circle. What can we say about forces that keep objects moving in circles? The most significant thing about objects moving in circles is that they are not moving in straight lines. This seems a trivial statement but it is the key to understanding circular motion.

To move at a constant speed in a straight line requires there to be no net force acting. (This is Newton's first law of motion.) When a mass moves in a circle it is constantly moving away from a straight line path and so there must be a net force acting. It is the force that forces the object away from its straight line motion. The force, called a **centripetal** (centre seeking) **force**, acts towards the centre of the circle and can be provided by any number of agents, including gravity, as shown in Figure 4.10.

The effect of a centripetal force is to change the velocity of a body by changing its direction. The speed itself doesn't change. Figure 4.11 shows the difference between the final velocity and the initial velocity following the action of a centripetal force. The change in velocity represents a **centripetal acceleration**. This is an acceleration without a change of speed, just a change in direction.

Velocity is a vector and has a magnitude (the speed) and a direction. Centripetal acceleration is a rate of change of velocity but only the directional part. The direction of the acceleration is parallel to the direction of the centripetal force, i.e. towards the centre of the circle.

(*Note:* The SLIPP unit *Physics for Sport* gives a comprehensive treatment of vectors.)

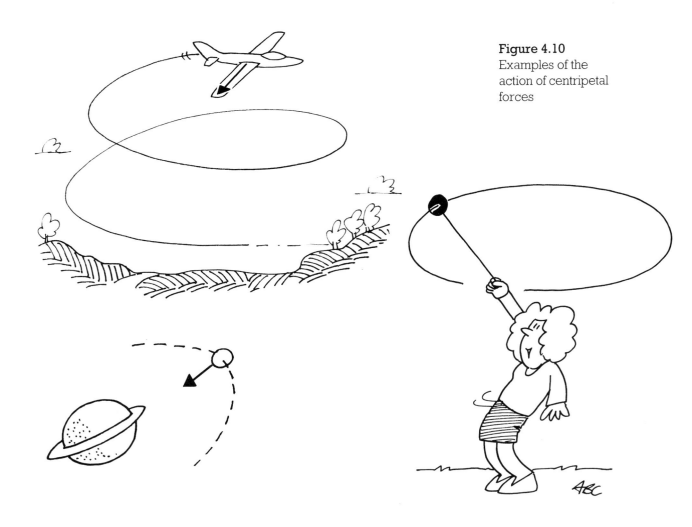

Figure 4.10
Examples of the
action of centripetal
forces

In Figure 4.11, a body, mass m, is moving in a circle with a speed v. The velocities are shown by bold type. (Note that the arrows have the same length but change direction.) The change in velocity from $\boldsymbol{v}_1$ to $\boldsymbol{v}_2$ is given by:

change in velocity = final velocity − initial velocity

$$= \boldsymbol{v}_2 - \boldsymbol{v}_1$$
$$= \boldsymbol{v}_2 + (-\boldsymbol{v}_1)$$

The difference between $\boldsymbol{v}_2$ and $\boldsymbol{v}_1$ is a change in velocity acting towards the centre of the circle.

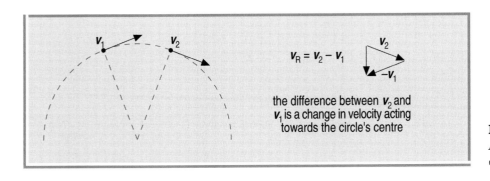

$$v_R = v_2 - v_1$$

the difference between v_2 and v_1 is a change in velocity acting towards the circle's centre

Figure 4.11
A body moving in a
circle

99

By drawing v_2 and v_1 as vectors using arrows we can show $v_2 + (-v_1)$ as a vector diagram. The result of the subtraction of these two vectors is the resultant vector, v_R. This acts towards the centre of the circle, in the same direction as the centripetal force.

 A cyclist is pedalling around a roundabout. The speed of the bike remains constant but the bike is accelerating. Explain this and give the direction of the acceleration

Acceleration is a change in velocity, a vector quantity. In this example the velocity changes in direction. This means the bike is accelerated – in a direction towards the centre of the roundabout.

From Newton's second law

force = mass × acceleration

$$F = m \times a$$

 If Newton says that a force is needed for any acceleration, what force makes the bike accelerate in the previous question?

On a flat road it would be the friction between the tyres and road. Some roads are banked to make the bike lean into the bend.

An expression exists to calculate the circular acceleration:

$$a = \frac{v^2}{r}$$

where r is the radius of the circle, giving us a way of determining the centripetal force from

$$F = \frac{m \times v^2}{r}$$

 Calculate the speed in km hr^{-1} of an orbiting satellite, mass 500 kg, that takes 4.0 hr to move once a4yund an orbit of radius 6000 km.

Circumference of a circle $= 2 \times \pi \times r$

where r is the radius of the circle

$$\text{speed} = \frac{\text{distance travelled}}{\text{time taken}}$$

$$= \frac{2 \times \pi \times r}{t}$$

$$= \frac{2 \times \pi \times 6000\,\text{km}}{4.0\,\text{hr}}$$

$$= 9.4 \times 10^3 \,\text{km hr}^{-1} \text{ or } 9400\,\text{km hr}^{-1} \text{ (to two significant figures)}$$

Calculate the size of the centripetal force that acts on the satellite in the above question and draw a free body force diagram of the satellite. (Remember to convert to SI units before doing the calculation.)

Centripetal force $= \dfrac{m \times v^2}{r}$

$$\dfrac{500\,\text{kg} \times \left(9400\,\text{km}\,\text{hr}^{-1}\right)^2}{6000\,\text{km}}$$

$$= \dfrac{500\,\text{kg} \times \left(9400 \times 1000\,\text{m} \times 3600\,\text{s}^{-1}\right)^2}{6000 \times 1000\,\text{m}}$$

$$= 5.7 \times 10^2\,\text{N or } 570\,\text{N (to two significant figures)}$$

The free body force diagram is shown in Figure 4.12.

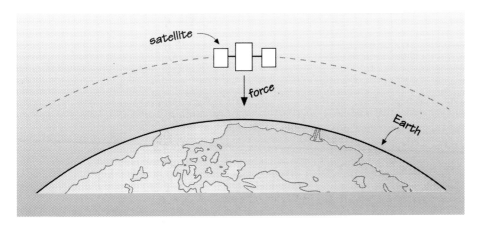

Figure 4.12
Free body force diagram

Q8 Calculate the size of the centripetal force needed to keep the following objects moving in a circle. In each case identify the cause of the centripetal force.

(a) A 0.20 kg bird moving in a circle of radius 20 m at a constant speed of 4.0 m s^{-1}.

(b) A child, mass 30 kg, standing on a playground roundabout, moving at 2.0 m s^{-1} in a circle of radius 2.0 m.

(c) An asteroid, mass 6.0×10^8 kg, moving at a speed of 21 000 m s^{-1} in a circle of radius 3.0×10^{11} m around the Sun. ◆

4.2 Universal gravitation

Of course, every apple on Newton's tree was attracted to Earth, as were the branches and Newton himself. He realized that whatever gravity was (and he couldn't really puzzle out what it was), it acted between Earth and all masses, including masses some height off Earth's surface, such as the Moon.

Newton calculated the centripetal acceleration of the Moon. He knew that the distance between the centres of Earth and Moon was about 380 000 km and the period, T, of the Moon's orbit was about 27.3 days.

Worked example

This worked example uses data to repeat Newton's calculation of the centripetal acceleration, v^2/r, of the Moon.

The first thing to do is to calculate the speed.

For an object moving in a circle:

$$\text{speed} = \frac{\text{circumference}}{\text{period}}$$

$$v = \frac{2\pi r}{T}$$

Using the values above (converted into SI units, i.e. metres and seconds) and using $\pi = 3.14$ we get

$$v = \frac{2 \times 3.14 \times \left(3.8 \times 10^8\right) \text{m}}{\left(27.3 \times 24 \times 3.6 \times 10^3\right) \text{s}}$$

$$= 1.0117 \times 10^3 \,\text{ms}^{-1}$$

$$= 1.0 \times 10^3 \,\text{ms}^{-1} \text{ (to two significant figures)}$$

The centripetal acceleration of the Moon is given by

$$a = \frac{v^2}{r}$$

$$= \frac{\left(1.0117 \times 10^3 \,\text{ms}^{-1}\right)^2}{3.8 \times 10^8 \,\text{m}}$$

$$= 2.6935 \times 10^3 \,\text{ms}^{-2}$$

$$= 2.7 \times 10^3 \,\text{ms}^{-2} \text{ (to two significant figures)} \quad \blacklozenge$$

Now, Newton knew that the value of gravitational acceleration of all falling objects on Earth's surface was 9.81 m s^{-2}. This value was far too large to match the Moon's acceleration. But Newton speculated that gravity could become diluted as it reached out into space. Perhaps it might just be 0.0027 m s^{-2} at a distance as far as the Moon. (See Figure 4.13.)

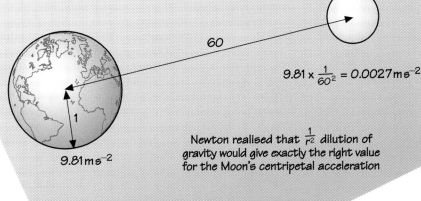

$$9.81 \times \frac{1}{60^2} = 0.0027 \, \text{ms}^{-2}$$

Newton realised that $\frac{1}{r^2}$ dilution of gravity would give exactly the right value for the Moon's centripetal acceleration

Figure 4.13
Moon's centripetal acceleration

He knew that the Moon was about 60 times further from Earth's centre than his apple was. Perhaps gravity becomes diluted by a factor of 60 by the time we reach the Moon. However $(1/60) \times 9.81$ m s^{-2} was still far too large.

 Try this calculation for yourself. Then try a dilution factor of $1/(60)^2$

$$\frac{1}{60} \times 9.81 \, \text{ms}^{-2} = 1.6 \times 10^{-1} \, \text{ms}^{-2}$$

which is too small, but

$$\frac{1}{60^2} \times 9.81 \, \text{ms}^{-2} = 2.7 \times 10^{-3} \, \text{ms}^{-2}$$

which is the right value.

The discovery of this inverse square relationship was a triumph for Newton. (Incidentally he had to invent a new type of mathematics called calculus in order to show that Earth's mass could be considered as being at the centre of Earth.) Out of this work came Newton's law of **universal gravitation**. Newton stated that gravitational attraction existed between all matter. Not only was it responsible for falling apples but also for the orbit of the Moon, for Jupiter's moons and indeed all the objects in the

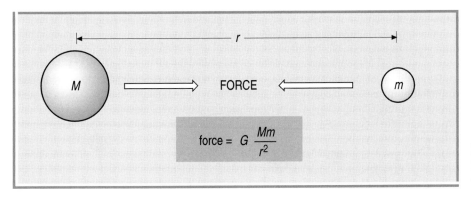

Figure 4.14
Newton's law of universal gravitation

103

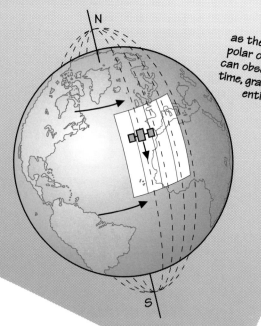

as the Earth turns, a polar orbiting satellite can observe a strip at a time, gradually seeing the entire surface

solar system. They all attract each other with a force that depends on the product of their masses and the square of the separation between their centres, as shown in Figure 4.14.

The constant in this equation is G, known as 'big G' to avoid confusion with 'g'.

Its value is 6.67×10^{-11} N m^2 kg^{-2}. The small value of G reflects just how weak gravitational forces are, as you found earlier in Section 2 on nuclear physics.

Spy satellites

Satellites that are designed to look at different locations on Earth's surface might typically have a security role or an environmental role. They need to be above different places at different times; for example, to compile whole world maps of land use or to look at shipping movements across the Pacific Ocean. Such satellites are called **polar orbiting** satellites and are never too far away, typically 800 km above Earth's surface. They are so close that you can see them pass overhead on a dark, clear night. They look like slow-moving stars taking about a minute to cross your field of view. The Space Shuttle is a low-orbit satellite. You can observe the passage of low orbiters with the help of newspaper prediction tables like the one shown in Figure 4.15.

The possibility of a low-orbit satellite emerged from Newton's thought experiment on the motion of canonballs. Newton's thought experiment went like this:

Satellite predictions

LONDON

	From	To	Max Elev	Rises/ Sets
Cosmos 1697R	17.12	17.19	50NNE	NNW/ESE
Erbs		18.24	18.27	48N	NW/*NE
Zenit		19.01	19.06	72NE	NNW/*ESE

MANCHESTER

	From	To	Max Elev	Rises/ Sets
Cosmos 1697R	17.11	17.19	53ENE	NNW/ESE
Erbs		18.23	18.27	60NE	WNW/*ENE
Zenit		19.00	19.06	69NNE	NNW/*ESE

*Leaves or enters eclipse. Predictions are for tomorrow.
Data supplied by the Royal Greenwich Observatory.

Figure 4.15
Polar orbiting satellite and prediction table

Figure 4.16
A cannonball fired from a hilltop

Imagine a canonball fired horizontally from a hilltop. It would fall to the ground some distance away. A second faster ball would fall further away but still follow a curved path (see Figure 4.16). A ball even faster might be so fast that it fell at a rate just matching the curvature of Earth. Such a ball would orbit Earth. All three balls would be pulled down towards Earth by gravity and so would be falling to Earth. In the third case Earth's surface would simply be curving away.

We describe all such falling objects as being in a state of **free fall**. A fourth ball dropped vertically down would also be forced by gravity and also be in free fall. The others just happen to be moving forward at the same time.

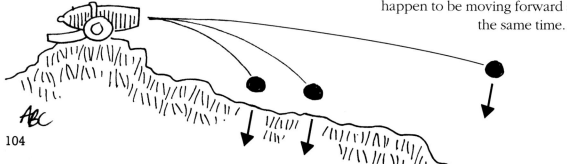

Exploration 4.1
Independence of vertical and horizontal acceleration

45 MINUTES

Part (i)

Apparatus:

◆ two tennis balls

Arrange for two objects, say tennis balls, to be dropped from a height of several metres, perhaps out of an upstairs window. Repeat the experiment but release one with a sideways speed while the other is just allowed to fall. Repeated attempts should allow you to release the two balls at the same time. They are both in free fall and should hit the ground simultaneously. Once released, the only forces acting on these objects will be gravity, acting vertically, and perhaps a little air resistance. If you do this outside and start the sideways ball with sufficient speed you will send it into orbit and it will return from behind you in about an hour. However, you would need a speed of about 8000 m s^{-1}!

You can do a more controlled experiment by following the instructions in Part (ii).

Part (ii)

Disinfect mouthpiece between use by different students.

Apparatus:

◆ cardboard cut-out shape attached to a right-angled soft iron bracket
◆ coil of 120 turns or a small electromagnet ◆ C-core ◆ low-voltage DC power supply ◆ two connecting leads about 3 m long ◆ marbles or steel balls about 1 to 1.5 cm diameter ◆ tube to project the marble (the marble must roll freely along it)
◆ flexible rubber mouthpiece to fit over the end of the tube ◆ four tall clamp stands, bosses and clamps ◆ thin strips of aluminium foil ◆ rod of insulating material, e.g. wooden dowel or stiff card

The apparatus should be set up as in Figure 4.17 overleaf. As a safety measure, use the small piece of rubber tubing as a mouthpiece on the blowing end of the tube. Dip the mouthpiece into some dilute disinfectant and rinse with water before another student uses it. Clip a thin strip of aluminium foil on to a rod of insulating material supported by a clamp stand. The foil is placed in the path of the marble so that when blown out of the tube the marble will break the contact. Keep the foil close to the end of the tube.

With the foil contact made and the circuit complete the cardboard shape will be held by the electromagnet. Use as low a current as you need to just hold the cardboard shape. The centre of the shape must be level with the height of the end of the tube.

When the foil is broken the circuit breaks and the cardboard shape will fall. Will your marble strike the shape even though the shape falls vertically and the marble follows a curved path?

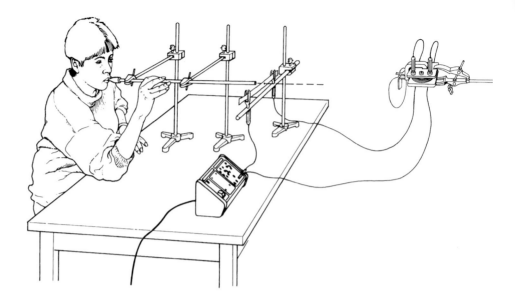

Figure 4.17
The set-up for Exploration 4.1

Communication satellites

TV satellite dishes are a common sight throughout the world. In the UK they are fixed to south-facing walls and tilt upwards at an angle of about 30°. The satellites that send these communications to Earth are also fixed – fixed in space located above a point on Earth's surface.

 If they are not moving, why don't these satellites fall down to Earth?

They are not stationary in an absolute sense. They are orbiting Earth but with a period of exactly one day.

Geostationary or (geosynchronous) satellites (Figure 4.18) remain in the same place relative to Earth. They orbit above the Equator. For a satellite to have a period of orbit of exactly 24 hours, it must have a radius of orbit $= 4.23 \times 10^7$ m. This places geostationary satellites at a height above Earth's surface of about 36 000 km, about six Earth radii away. Their speed is such that they must cover the 260 000 km orbit in 24 hours. The idea that such satellites were possible was first proposed by Arthur C. Clarke, a science fiction writer, in 1947! So to find out what will happen tomorrow read sci-fi today!

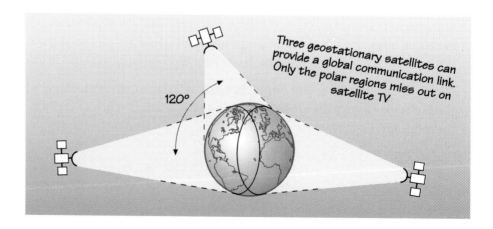

Figure 4.18
Geostationary satellites

To calculate the orbital height of a geostationary satellite we start with an equation relating the centripetal force to the gravitational attraction:

centripetal force = gravitational attraction for a mass m in orbit around a body of mass M

$$\frac{GMm}{r^2} = \frac{mv^2}{r}$$

$$\frac{GM}{r} = v^2 \qquad (4.2)$$

but for a geostationary satellites in orbit around Earth:

$$v = \frac{2 \times \pi \times r}{T} \qquad (4.3)$$

where T is the orbital period (24×3600 s). So, substituting for v in Equation (4.2) gives

$$\frac{GM}{r} = \frac{4\pi^2 r^2}{T^2} \qquad (4.4)$$

Putting in the values

$$G = 6.67 \times 10^{-11} \ \text{Nm}^2 \ \text{kg}^{-2}$$

$$M = 6.0 \times 10^{24} \ \text{kg}$$

and

$$T = 24 \times 3600 \, \text{s}$$

gives

$$\frac{\left(6.67 \times 10^{-11} \ \text{Nm}^2 \ \text{kg}^{-2}\right) \times \left(6.0 \times 10^{24} \ \text{kg}\right)}{r} = \frac{4 \times \pi^2 \times r^2}{\left(24 \times 3600 \, \text{s}\right)^2}$$

therefore

$$r^3 = \frac{\left(6.67 \times 10^{-11} \ \text{Nm}^2 \ \text{kg}^{-2}\right) \times \left(6.0 \times 10^{24} \ \text{kg}\right) \times \left(24 \times 3600 \, \text{s}\right)^2}{4 \times \pi^2}$$

$$= 7.567 \times 10^{22} \ \text{m}^3$$

and

$$r = 4.23 \times 10^7 \ \text{m}$$

The moons of Jupiter

With the aid of his new telescope Galileo recorded the positions of the four bright moons of Jupiter over several nights. He realized that the moons were in orbit around Jupiter. The chart in Figure 4.19 shows the motion of the four large Galilean moons, Io, Europa, Ganymede and Callisto over a period of a few weeks.

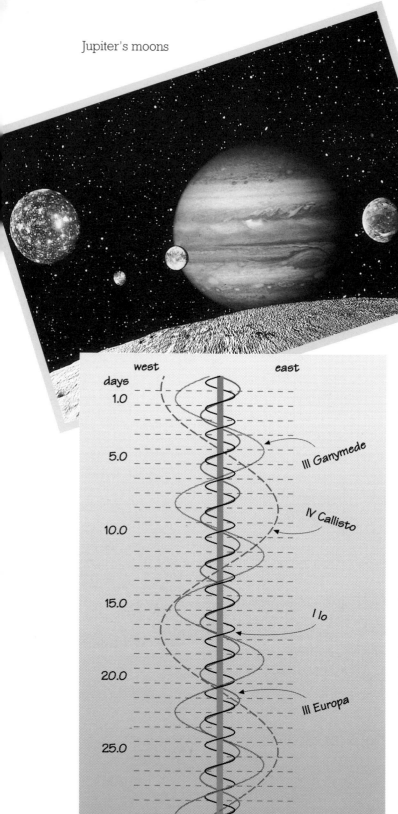

Q9 Use Figure 4.19 to find the period of (a) Io, (b) Europa, (c) Ganymede, (d) Callisto. ◆

Johannes Kepler, a contemporary of Galileo living in Germany, proposed that there was a relationship between the period of a planet and the radius of its orbit. Based on the evidence provided by Danish observer Tycho Brahe, Kepler suggested that for the planets:

$$\frac{\text{radius}^3}{\text{period}^2} = \text{constant}$$

This is known as Kepler's third law. It was an **empirical** statement – one based on observations. Newton used his law of universal gravitation to derive the same expression mathematically. This is how it was done:

From Equation (4.4)

$$\frac{r^3}{T^2} = \frac{GM}{4\pi^2}$$

the left-hand side of this expression is a constant for all satellites in orbit about a body of mass M.

Figure 4.19
The motion of Jupiter's moons

Q10 Use your answers to Question 9 and the data in Table 4.1 for Jupiter's Galilean satellites to find a mean value for the constant $\frac{r^3}{T^2}$ in $\text{km}^3 \, \text{d}^{-2}$. ◆

Table 4.1 Data for Question 10

Satellite	Orbital radius/km
Io	422 000
Europe	671 000
Ganymede	1 070 000
Callisto	1 880 000

Q11 Since Galileo's discoveries, a number of smaller satellites have been discovered in orbit around Jupiter. One, Himalia, was found to have an orbit of radius 11.5×10^6 km. Use your data and Kepler's third law to calculate the period of orbit for Himalia. ◆

Exploring the solar system

The launch of *Sputnik 1* by the Soviet Union in 1957 started the exploration of the solar system. There have been probes to the Moon, Mercury, Venus, Mars and Jupiter. American *Voyager* probes charted and photographed the outermost reaches of the solar system, there has been a rendezvous with Halley's Comet followed by the Galileo mission photographing the asteroids and then sending a probe into Jupiter.

 Exploration 4.2 A research activity

Find out what is currently happening in space. Which missions are reaching the national press, who is supporting them and what are the objectives? Is there much happening to forge international collaboration? Look at the popular science press. *New Scientist* and *Astronomy Now* are available in libraries and good newsagents. The Internet holds pages containing NASA information and much more (see the Further Reading and Resources section for the NASA web site address). Prepare a single side of A4 in the form of a space update newsletter; perhaps something that could be included on a student information noticeboard of a college magazine.

With each of these missions space technology has advanced a little further. But one important feature of all such space journeys remains – the problem of leaving Earth – the launch.

Launching a space probe is just a matter of energy transfer (in theory)

Fortunately for space physicists, Earth's gravitational field strength reduces with distance. Newton's universal law showed that this reduction or 'dilution' changes as $1/r^2$, which means that in launching a space vehicle most of the energy is transferred in leaving Earth's surface and moving away through our local space, a few Earth diameters away. Figure 4.20 shows how Earth's gravitational field weakens and also how the energy transformed in moving a 1 kg mass between two places decreases the further you are from the centre of Earth. The total area under the curve represents the energy required for a 1 kg mass to escape completely from Earth's gravitational influence. This is a fixed amount and is known as the **escape energy** per kilogram. Earth's escape energy is about 6.6×10^7 J kg^{-1}. You can estimate this from the area under the graph in Figure 4.20 by counting the squares and multiplying by the energy represented by each square.

To send a 1 kg mass into space with a speed so great that, even though Earth's gravity would be forcing it to slow down, it would continue to infinity, the 1 kg mass would need to transform 6.6×10^7 J of energy. A space probe with mass 1000 kg would transform 1000 times this energy. The simplest way of giving a mass this energy would be to give it kinetic

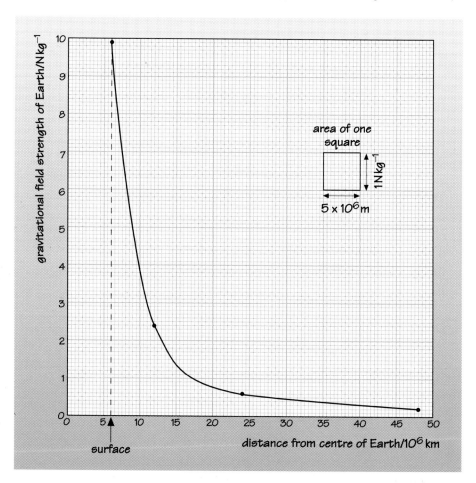

Figure 4.20
Gravitational field strength of Earth

energy and then let it move freely away from Earth transferring the kinetic energy to gravitational potential energy. An object with less than the escape energy would eventually fall back to Earth (what goes up must come down). However, an object with more than the escape energy would never return. To have just enough kinetic energy to allow a 1 kg mass to escape to infinity it needs to be moving initially at a particular velocity: the **escape velocity**.

The escape velocity for a mass m can be calculated from the escape energy per kg:

kinetic energy per kg = escape energy per kg

$$\frac{\frac{1}{2}mv^2}{m} = 6.6 \times 10^7 \, \mathrm{J\,kg^{-1}}$$

So

$$\frac{1}{2}v^2 = 6.6 \times 10^7 \, \mathrm{J\,kg^{-1}}$$

therefore

$$v^2 = 2 \times 6.6 \times 10^7 \, \mathrm{J\,kg^{-1}}$$

so

$$v = \sqrt{2 \times 6.6 \times 10^7 \, \mathrm{m^2\,s^{-2}}}$$

$$= 11489 \, \mathrm{m\,s^{-1}}$$

$$= 1.1 \times 10^4 \, \mathrm{m\,s^{-1}} \text{ or } 11000 \, \mathrm{m\,s^{-1}} \text{ (to two significant figures)}$$

This escape velocity is the same for every object. So a 0.2 kg apple and a 150 kg satellite would both need to reach a velocity of $11\,000$ m s^{-1} in order to escape to infinity.

 Suggest how might you accelerate an object to a velocity of $11\,000$ m s^{-1}.

A large rubber band? Light blue touch paper and retire? Place an explosive mixture under it? Impact with a well swung golf club? These are all energy transfer mechanisms known to science.

 If this could be achieved in a short time, say 10 s, the speeding mass would be moving through Earth's atmosphere at $11\,000$ m s^{-1} on the first part of its journey into deep space. What effect would this have on the object?

It would most probably burn up through frictional heating. It would also be subject to a large drag force from air resistance, which would remove much of its kinetic energy. If it were not to burn up altogether it would eventually fall back to Earth.

Rocket fuel has its own mass. If the combustion energy in 1 kg of rocket fuel is exactly 6.6×10^7 J, how might this affect the launch of a deep space probe?

The fuel would barely get itself into deep space let alone the mass of the rocket. This is a big problem for space scientists.

Most of the mass of a rocket is the fuel. Fuel technology is such that at present no fuel can provide enough energy per kg to accelerate itself and a payload to a speed of 11 000 m s^{-1} to attain a complete escape. Other techniques need to be adopted.

Nothing is stationary in space. A rocket standing on a launch pad is moving, as indeed are we all, because we are on a spinning Earth. A rocket ready for launch from a site such as Kourou in French Guiana is near the Equator and so already has a speed of about 440 m s^{-1}. A rocket ready for launch at Cape Canaveral will be moving at 405 m s^{-1}. Such launches give rockets a free boost of speed even before countdown.

A rocket launched from any site on Earth has also the speed of Earth's orbit around the Sun. This is a free speed of about 30 000 m s^{-1}. The rocket engines on a typical launch can add a further 7000 m s^{-1}.

Clearly the two main components determining the speed of a launched probe are the rockets and Earth's solar orbit. However, the direction of launch will either cause these velocities to add or to subtract. The result is that two types of solar orbit are possible. Both are known as Hohmann orbits and they are both elliptical. When the rockets add to Earth's solar orbital motion the final probe will move at about 37 000 m s^{-1} and will move beyond Earth orbit towards Mars orbit. If the rockets launch the probe in the opposite sense to Earth's solar orbit the final launch speed will be about 23 000 m s^{-1} and this will result in an orbit that takes the probe towards Venus. (See Figure 4.21.) In all Hohmann orbits the orbital path returns the vehicle to the original launch location.

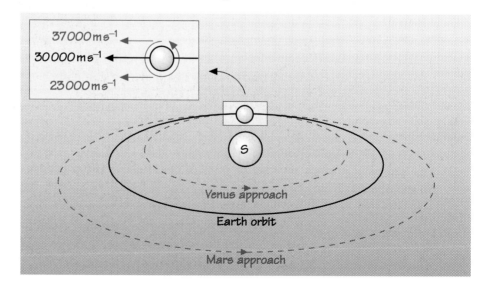

Figure 4.21
Hohmann orbits

Galileo mission to Jupiter

The *Galileo* probe was launched from Earth by the Space Shuttle *Atlantis* in October 1989. Its journey is shown in Figure 4.22. The energy per kilogram required to place *Atlantis* and *Galileo* in low Earth orbit is around 10% of the energy needed to escape. This is easily achievable with existing rocket fuel technology.

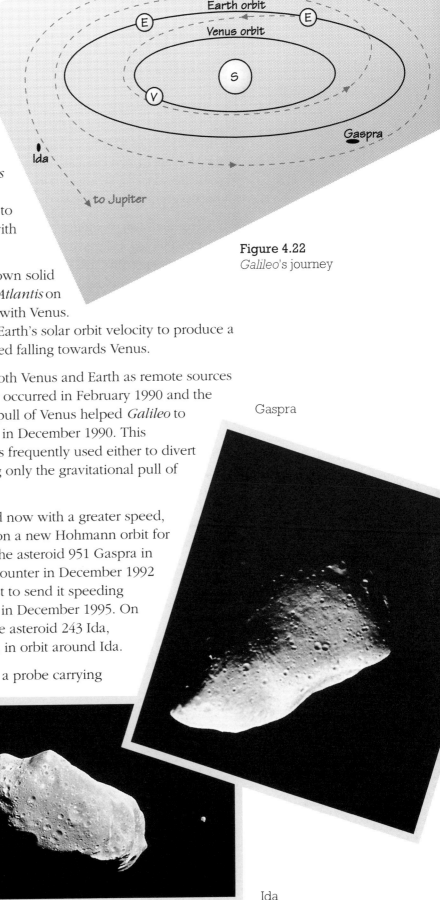

Figure 4.22
Galileo's journey

Galileo, with the assistance of its own solid rocket boosters, left Space Shuttle *Atlantis* on 18 October 1989 for a rendezvous with Venus. Its own rocket was acting against Earth's solar orbit velocity to produce a slow Hohmann orbit; *Galileo* started falling towards Venus.

Galileo was programmed to use both Venus and Earth as remote sources of kinetic energy. The Venus flyby occurred in February 1990 and the forward motion and gravitational pull of Venus helped *Galileo* to accelerate onwards to fly by Earth in December 1990. This technique, called **gravity assist**, is frequently used either to divert or to speed up space probes using only the gravitational pull of the moving planets.

Gaspra

Following the first Earth flyby, and now with a greater speed, *Galileo* headed out beyond Mars on a new Hohmann orbit for a photographic rendezvous with the asteroid 951 Gaspra in October 1991. A second Earth encounter in December 1992 gave *Galileo* a further gravity assist to send it speeding outwards for its Jupiter encounter in December 1995. On the way, *Galileo* photographed the asteroid 243 Ida, discovering a tiny satellite, Dactyl, in orbit around Ida.

On 7 December 1995 *Galileo* sent a probe carrying instruments to sample atmospheric conditions to parachute through Jupiter's clouds. The latest progress of *Galileo* can be found on the NASA Internet site (see the Further Reading and Resources section).

Ida

4.3 Public science – Comet Shoemaker–Levy 9

The space in which we live is seething with gravitational fields. Normally the gravitational field due to the Sun (a thousand times more massive than all the planets put together) dominates. The orbiting planets and asteroids describe more or less circular orbits about the Sun. Comets, wanderers from the icy depths, swing periodically into the inner solar system on highly eccentric ellipses focused on the Sun.

But occasionally an incoming comet will get close enough to a planet to get trapped in its local gravitational field, and never make it to the Sun. So it was with Comet Shoemaker–Levy 9 (SL9). Caught by Jupiter up to 100 years ago, it flew so close to the giant planet in July 1992 that jovian gravity simply ripped it apart.

For the next two years, more than 20 fragments of SL9 swept out to 50 million kilometres away from Jupiter before finally hurtling in to crash into the planet during the week of 16–22 July 1994. The enormous resulting explosions, clearly visible to astronomers' large telescopes, were beamed around the world by the television networks and appeared on the front pages of newspapers.

Thanks to the 15 months advanced notice of SL9's demise, astronomers were well prepared for the event. So were the media. As well as carrying scientific information about the event – predicted and eventually measured – a number of other themes were used to make the story attractive to the public. These ranged from cosmic impacts to explain the extinction of the dinosaurs, to comets as portents of doom.

Read the accompanying articles from the *Daily Telegraph* and the *Guardian*.

As a comit hurtles towards a nearby planet, Science Editor **Roger Highfield** previews the biggest impact in modern astronomy

Crash course for Jupiter

THE crash of a comet into Jupiter next month, one of the most widely anticipated events in the history of modern astronomy, can already be witnessed thanks to simulations carried out in powerful computers.

From July 16 onwards, mountain-sized fragments of the comet will hurtle into Jupiter's upper atmosphere to trigger an explosion equivalent to 100 million megatons of TNT.

"These objects are about two to four kilometres across," said Hubble Space Telescope scientist Dr Ed Weiler. "The best theory of what destroyed the dinosaurs on Earth about 65 million years ago was that just one object about this size fell into the atmosphere and messed things up."

The newly refurbished Hubble Space Telescope will be one of many gazing at the spectacle, along with a host of other Earth-orbiting and interplanetary spacecraft.

Even amateur astronomers may see some effects when the fragments smash into Jupiter like bullets from a cosmic machine gun.

"This is the first time we've been able to predict a major impact and then prepare to observe it scientifically," said Dr Gene Shoemaker, a US Geological Survey scientist and co-discoverer of the Shoemaker Levy 9 comet.

Astronomers have known since the spring of 1993 that its fragments will hit Jupiter this summer – it broke into at least 21 pieces during its last close encounter with the planet in July 1992, when giant Jovian "tidal" forces ripped it apart.

This page offers a preview of what to expect. A team at Sandia National Laboratories in New Mexico used the 1,840 processors in the world's fastest supercomputer, the Intel Paragon, to learn more about the fireball that is created when a fragment enters Jupiter's atmosphere.

Using computer programs originally developed to model nuclear weapon blast effects, Sandia scientists began calculating the effects of a two-mile diameter fragment – one large enough to deliver about six million megatons of energy.

One simulation focuses on the disintegration of the fragment in the Jovian atmosphere, the second on the resulting fireball that will create temperatures more than half that of the Sun's surface. Each impact will be separated by a few hours.

"This astronomical event is unprecedented. Never before has an object been discovered, its orbit calculated, and an impact prediction made. This allows astronomers a unique observational opportunity and provides a similarly unique opportunity for us to validate our computer code," Dr David Crawford of Sandia said.

The second type of computer simulation, carried out on a 512 processor nCUBE 2 computer by a group of planetary scientists at the Massachusetts Institute of Technology, shows the collisions' effect on Jupiter's weather by calculating the effects on the atmosphere.

Calculated using 400 hours of computer time by Dr Joseph Harrington, Mr Raymond LeBeau, Ms Kari Backes, and Prof Timothy Dowling, all of MIT's Department of Earth, Atmospheric, and Planetary Sciences, the simulations show waves travelling outward from the impact sites and travelling around the planet in the days following each impact.

The waves are surface waves, large motions of the atmosphere that are similar to ripples on a pond. Dr Harrington, Prof Dowling, and Dr Heidi Hammel, also of MIT, will observe the real impacts with the Hubble Space Telescope and the Nasa Infrared Telescope Facility in Hawaii.

By comparing the real thing with their simulations, they hope to measure the wave speeds and thus determine characteristics of the planet's atmosphere more accurately. Better-known parameters will improve understanding of planetary weather systems.

Dr Harrington said estimates of energy released on impact could be out by a factor of 400, the size of the objects being the biggest unknown in the calculation. "The Hubble telescope observers recently revised their size estimates downward, after receiving new data from the refurbished telescope. They unfortunately have not stated hard numbers, but have said the sizes could be no larger than their previous estimates, and may be smaller."

Early estimates predicted the fragments would hit the planet just beyond the visible horizon as seen from Earth, producing flashes so bright that the light will reflect off Jupiter's moons. Since Jupiter spins rapidly, the impact points will rotate into telescope sighting within minutes.

"There might be something visible to Earth, certainly not to the naked eye but to a telescope in certain wavelength regions, such as the infrared," Dr Crawford said.

"The worst case would be if they all disappear and there is no effect," Dr Shoemaker said, "but I will be astonished if we don't see something."

He added that the cosmic collision is a reminder of the remote, but real, danger that such a comet could smash into the Earth with devastating effect.

(*Daily Telegraph*, 29 June 1994)

Serial killers from heaven

On July 16 at around 9pm at least 20 fragments of a comet called Shoemaker–Levy 9 will starting slamming in to the far side of Jupiter. What does it mean for earthlings? **Tim Radford** on the celestial game of pinball

COMETS WERE once regarded as prodigies – things to be wondered at – and portents of change. They still are, says Dr Victor Clube, an astrophysicist at Oxford. He says that anyone on Earth has a one in four chance during a lifetime of being affected in some way by something falling from the sky. He says that fireballs from heaven play a bigger part in human history than most people are prepared to recognise. When he and his colleague Dr Bill Napier first started saying things like this in books like their latest, The Cosmic Winter (Blackwell 1990) – they were regarded as somewhat dodgy customers.

But the picture has changed. Several groups of American space scientists have been talking about the "Chicken Little" syndrome. Chicken Little was the hen in the nursery books who thought the sky was falling in. But the sky is falling in, and people in high places are prepared to believe it.

Two scientists from Arizona and California this year calculated that there was a one in 10,000 chance of a 2km diameter comet or asteroid colliding with the Earth in the next century, killing a very large section of humanity. A third calculated that the chances of death from an asteroid was about the same as death in an airline accident. This school of thought is called catastrophism. It argues that the

planet, and with it the solar system, are not as they are because of the slow accretion of processes over time: they are also subject to periodic and catastrophic bumps.

The idea – heretical for a while – re-emerged after the discovery of a massive smash of a large extra-terrestrial object into the Yucatan peninsula in Mexico, about 65 million years ago, co-incident with the end of the dinosaurs, and about 80 per cent of all other life then on Earth. It is now accepted that the same thing may have happened four times, in earlier periods. The difference between Victor Clube and the others is that he has been saying it louder and for longer.

"I don't want to sound as though I am blowing my own trumpet: I'm a long standing catastrophist, long before anybody else knew about it. We even wrote something about the dinosaurs being bumped off before the great discovery," he says The "we" includes, as always, his co-author Bill Napier, who describes the partnership as "the Morecambe and Wise of astrophysics".

But what Clube and Napier have to say still causes offence. "You could label me as such an extreme catastrophist that I make most catastrophists uncomfortable," Clube says. "I am not doing it out of sheer cussedness: there is a straightforward rational thesis for everything that is being said."

The essence of his argument is this: that it is dangerous out there. The solar system is a kind of series of M25s, across which articulated lorries come careering, out of the blue and out of control; in which the innocent planet burbling along safely on the inside lane might find itself one day narrowly missing a Mercedes Unimog, and then on another outing perceive no hazard at all, and on the third find bouncing towards it several crates of machine tools spilled from a Scania trailer.

The Shoemaker–Levy collision with Jupiter is an example, he says. A few years ago, it was just a comet that was orbiting Jupiter, more or less predictably. Then, on its 1992 approach, it was subjected to gravitational strains that broke it up. It's easy to break up a comet, he says: they are agglomerations of ice and rock, loosely assembled, like a sandcastle. But once fractured, it became so much less predictable. Instead of a single body in a single orbit, there are now 20 bits of rock, all in very slightly different orbits, ready to rain down upon the planet in sequence, like mortar bombs, each with the explosive power of the most powerful thermonuclear warheads known to man.

But first, the game of pinball in the solar system. There is the Sun, and the nine planets with their moons, and what is usually thought to be a planet that never happened in the asteroid belt between Mars and Jupiter. And then there is the zodiacal cloud, a sheet of dust and small stones more or less in the plane of the planets. And then, far beyond Pluto, extending halfway to the nearest star, is the Oort Cloud, where the comets live.

About 700 comets have been recorded by historians and astronomers, and new ones turn up at the rate of about five per year. But out there in the Oort cloud, there could be 100 billion or 1,000 billion comets, each with an average mass of 10 billion or 100 billion tons. Every now and then, one or two more get dislodged from their distant orbits, and battle into the solar system, to be captured by the gravitational pull of the Sun, or a large planet like Jupiter.

Why this happens is not clear. Some years ago there was talk of an invisible companion star to the Sun. It was called Nemesis because, for some time now, science has become aware of rhythmic evidence of extreme violence done to the Earth and other planets. The rocks of the Earth are a kind of history book in which the serial development of life is inscribed. Every so often in the strata, there are sudden cessations of life, a kind of sharp line drawn, after which new creatures appear in the fossil record. There are periods, too, of mountain building, and sudden climate change. The guess has been that some extraterrestrial agency may have been at work. Clube is not keen on the Nemesis idea.

"Such systems are highly unstable and all astrophysicists know it. Nothing would ever come back with that regularity, even if it were there. Nemesis is up the creek: there is still a periodicity and there is an obvious one."

The Sun rotates around the centre of the galaxy at roughly 220km a second. But, he says, it has a second velocity as well, of about 7km a second, out of the plane of the galaxy and back again. That is, the galaxy is a kind of enormous merry-go-round and the stars are slowly bobbing up and down like fairground horses. This means that not only is there a force on the Sun from the centre of the galaxy but, when it is riding high, from everywhere else in the galaxy as well.

"Here comes the difficult part: Bill Napier and I are still trying to write a proper paper on it. Essentially there is a galactic tide; not only is there a force pulling on the Sun, there is a tidal force pulling on it as well. This tide is enough to produce a differential force across the solar system so that

comets attached to the Sun feel slightly different forces from it."

The comets in the Oort cloud are gravitationally bound to the Sun. The force could detach them in the direction of another star or send them spinning into the centre of the solar system, and to their eventual doom. They pitch into the Sun, or a planet, or the moon of a planet, or they break up, and scatter about the solar system like a cloud of heavy buckshot.

At that point, they become really dangerous. Napier and Clube see the comets as the serial killers, not simply of prehistory, but of history as well. Every June and November, the Earth's orbit takes it through a stream of what may well be cometary rubble called the Taurids. Most people aren't conscious of bombardment from space but, nevertheless, 10,000 tons of dust and pebbles slam into the planet every year. Most of it is small, most of it is incinerated in the upper atmosphere. But every so often perhaps once a century along comes something 100 metres or so across, at maybe 70km a second, and behaves like a thermonuclear warhead. The most famous this century, occurred in Siberia in 1908: about 10km above the empty forests there was an explosion of 20 megatons.

Clube thinks such events are more common than anyone realises. They have a role in destroying, if not lives, then civilisations. He and Napier have been studying Chinese and monkish records, and calculated that every few hundred years, there is a huge rise in the number of fireballs blazing across the skies. These seem to parallel turning points in history: moments of famine and fear and bloodshed: the Dark Ages, the Reformation, the French revolution. He is convinced that periodic fears of the end of the world are connected to these heavenly bursts of fire. He points out that the very word "revolution" had, before the present sense of popular upheaval,

an astronomical one. Cromwell knew this: he described his own times as "God's revolution".

"Very roughly, these events are happening every 300 years. We have gone a couple of hundred years without anything happening, that's why we are so ruddy ignorant at the present time. That doesn't mean it is going to happen tomorrow, or in 10 years' time, or in 100 years' time, but if you are reasonable you will educate people into recognising that there is a one in four lifetime chance for everybody alive today."

He says that nobody in the astrophysical community seems to want to know about this. He says that even the old Star Wars people who are keeping the Chicken Little thesis bubbling in the United States are missing the point. Even the new catastrophists think that, essentially, the world is safe: if they had the instruments to detect asteroid or comet visitors, and the know-how to deflect them, everything would remain stable. Clube's point is that the heavenly serial killers are entirely unpredictable. The sudden conversion two years ago of Shoemaker–Levy 9 from a predictable periodic visitor into a shower of megaton buckshot destined this time to smack into its target proves that.

"The fact of collisions in space is recognised, but the message that scientists are trying to get across to the public is that they don't matter," he says. "I think this is wrong, I think it is immoral, it's disgustingly wrong. But there is a problem: what do you do about it? If you go round standing on a soap box and shout your head off, that the world is coming to an end, you are classified as a nutcase, and if you are a nutcase you are a nutcase, it is as simple as that. If it is rational, and you still want to say that, then it turns out to be a problem. How do you communicate the ruddy knowledge?"

(Guardian, 7 July 1994)

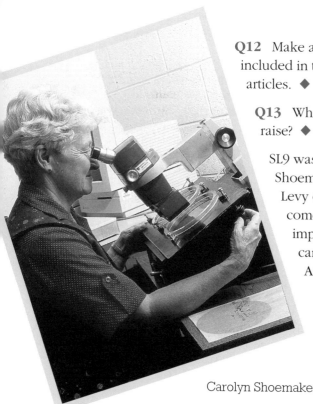

Carolyn Shoemaker

Q12 Make a list of: (a) four facts in the articles, (b) four predictions included in the articles, (c) four uses of technology mentioned in the articles. ◆

Q13 What social, historical and cultural issues does each article raise? ◆

SL9 was discovered by veteran comet watcher Carolyn Shoemaker, her husband Eugene and their colleague David Levy on 23 March 1993. Shoemaker–Levy 9 was the ninth comet they discovered together, and by far the most important. The following interview with Carolyn was carried out at the US Geological Survey in Flagstaff, Arizona, shortly after the collision with Jupiter occurred.

Interview with Carolyn Shoemaker

One of the questions that always comes up is whether scientists feel that they and their work has been well represented by the media. How do you feel about this?

For the most part, I think that the media did a pretty good job. The amount of attention I got was a totally new experience for me, however. A lot of the coverage started around February 1994, when Gene and I were in Australia and we were interviewed for their TV programme *60 minutes*.

So from March onwards, when we got back, it started in the US too, getting busier and busier through April, May and June so that all it seemed we did was deal with the media for several months, Gene on one phone and me on another. I think there were times when we felt that we were being pushed pretty hard by some of the interviewers, and then we would get tired.

We had gone to Baltimore so we could watch the images being taken by the Hubble Space Telescope. We were so lucky with those – the telescope had been repaired, the comet hit only just on the back side of Jupiter so we could see all the effects at the side of the planet. It was incredibly exciting – everyone felt the comet had performed well. But without doubt, as far as the media was concerned, that was the toughest week.

Did you find that you resented the media for preventing you from getting on with your research work?

No. Although it was cutting across our work, we felt above all that we had a responsibility to do this because it was important for astronomy as a whole and because the public was deeply interested in the impact. I think it is too bad if scientists do not speak up about the new discoveries and the new possibilities, because that way you get a lot more people interested and you get a lot more research done.

All science needs the public. If the public isn't interested then Congress isn't interested and they don't vote the funds necessary for research. Look at the Apollo Program. Enthusiasm for that died down much quicker than we ever anticipated and, as a result, that kind of manned space exploration died. So one of my enthusiasms for SL9 was that it got the public interest necessary to get the funding for a lot of good science.

Personally, I find anyway that I am much more comfortable talking to a general audience than giving a scientific lecture. I like to talk to amateur astronomy groups especially, because they are so terribly enthusiastic. But it was certainly tiring talking to the media and so many people. So, overall, my reaction to the attention we got has been mixed.

Do you think this episode demonstrates that scientists have wider responsibilities to the public? Is there a 'right to know?' For instance, what would you have done if you had found SL9 heading for Earth rather than Jupiter?

First of all, I would have made sure it was named after someone else!

But seriously, we would have handled it in the same way, I think. We would have contacted the Minor Planets Centre and got our colleagues to check its orbit, because – initially – you do not know what its orbit is going to be. And once you do that, and the results start getting round by email and so on, then news is bound to get out to the public.

If the comet was confirmed to be heading our way, we might want to try and blow it up or head it off course. And then the public had better know all about it, because there you are getting into the realm of politics. My biggest worry is about what the politicians might do. Countries would have to work in a spirit of co-operation because otherwise one country might say to another: 'Oh, you are going to change its course so it won't hit your country. So just who are you going to drop it on?'

As a result of SL9, Congress has set up a new committee with a brief to work out ways of detecting all comets and asteroids bigger than one kilometre across which might pose a threat to Earth. Personally, I am a little cynical about how long Congress's enthusiasm for this will last. But the first step is to find out what is there and then decide if we need to be concerned.

Has SL9 raised astronomical and scientific issues of general importance, in your opinion?

Well, we certainly wanted people to be aware that rocks do, occasionally, fall out of the sky and make a difference here on Earth. We have been carrying out work on the cratering record, but geologists and anthropologists do not readily accept what we find.

Secondly, I think it has demonstrated that the sky is a marvellous thing to study, to know about and be familiar with. When we look at the stars, they can be good friends. The sky can give perspective to our everyday lives. It's a little humbling to realize the enormity of space and how small we are on our little planet. But space is not always calm and peaceful, just as we have our troubles here on Earth.

Q14 Carolyn Shoemaker wanted the public to know about SL9. Briefly explain her reasons for this position. ◆

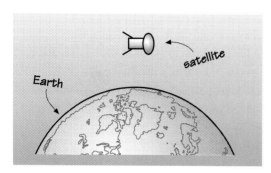

Figure 4.23
A satellite orbiting Earth

Q15 Figure 4.23 shows a satellite in polar orbit around Earth.

(a) Copy the satellite from the figure and using arrows indicate the direction of any forces acting on it.

(b) A video sequence from inside the satellite showed an astronaut appearing to 'float' in space. Explain why astronauts are able to do this.

(c) In order to rotate the satellite it is necessary for a small booster rocket to eject a gas into space for a short time. In this case a force of 400 N acted for 8.0 s. (i) Explain how the ejection of a gas can have an effect on the satellite. (ii) Calculate the magnitude of the impulse on the satellite as a result of this gas burst. (iii) If the impulse were to have had the effect of rotating the satellite, explain why a second impulse would be needed shortly after. ◆

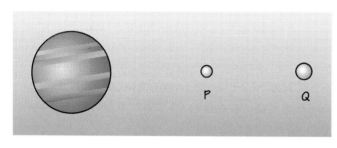

Figure 4.24
Two cometary fragments approaching Jupiter

Q16 Figure 4.24 shows two cometary fragments approaching the planet Jupiter.

P, mass 2000 kg, is at a distance 2.0×10^8 km and Q, mass 4000 kg, is at a distance 4.0×10^8 km from the centre of Jupiter.

(a) Show that the gravitational force between Jupiter and P is twice that which acts between Q and Jupiter.

(b) P and Q are both moving towards Jupiter on a collision course. Describe what will happen to the distance between P and Q as they approach Jupiter. Explain your answer.

(c) Figure 4.25 shows how the gravitational field strength varies with distance from the surface of Jupiter. (i) What is meant by 'gravitational field strength'? (ii) What shape is this curve? (iii) Explain how you could use the curve to calculate the gain in kinetic energy of a 1 kg mass as it fell from 400×10^6 km to 100×10^6 km. ◆

Q17 Figure 4.26 shows two extreme positions of Titan, Saturn's largest moon. The sketches were made eight days apart. The diameter of Saturn's ring system is 600 000 km

(a) Explain why Titan moves in a circular path.

(b) From Figure 4.26 estimate: (i) the orbital period of Titan, (ii) the orbital radius of Titan. Hence calculate (iii) the orbital speed of Titan, (iv) the centripetal acceleration of Titan.

(c) It can be shown that for all satellites orbiting a body, mass M, at a radius r

$$\frac{r^3}{T^2} = \frac{GM}{4\pi^2}$$

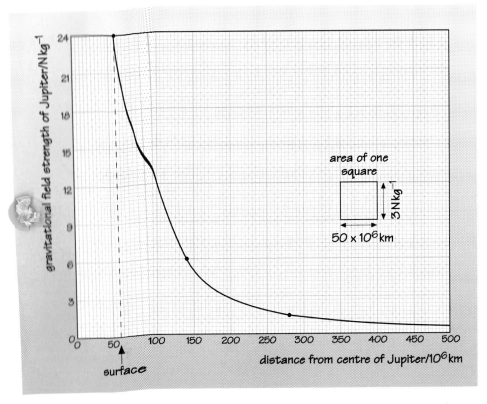

Figure 4.25
Graph of gravitational field strength varying with distance from the surface of Jupiter

Use this relationship together with the data from (b) to calculate a value for the mass of Saturn. (Use $G = 6.7 \times 10^{-11}$ N m^2 kg^{-2}.) ◆

Q18 The Moon is approximately 60 Earth radii away from the centre of Earth. Newton realized that the force responsible for attracting the Moon was the same force that acted on earthly objects like apples.

The centripetal acceleration of the Moon is 0.0027 m s^{-2}.

(a) Show that this value matches that which you would expect from Newton's law of universal gravitation.

(b) If the Moon is accelerating just like an apple, explain why it doesn't fall down and land on Earth.

(c) A common statement made by young children is 'There is no gravity on the Moon. This is because there is no atmosphere.' Is this statement true? Can you offer an alternative statement about gravity, atmosphere and the Moon that is correct. ◆

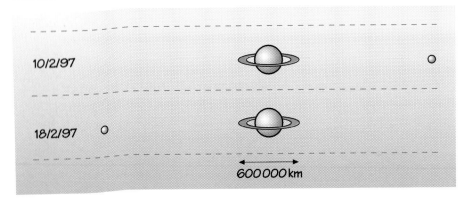

Figure 4.26
Titan orbiting Saturn

Achievements

After working through this section you should be able to:

- calculate an impulse and its effect
- describe the concept of universal gravitation and apply it to everyday and astronomical situations
- describe the role of a centripetal force and calculate the magnitude of a force for circular motion
- use the term 'free fall' to explain the motion of a natural or artificial satellite
- apply Kepler's third law to the motion of satellites using $F = \dfrac{GMm}{r^2}$ and $a = \dfrac{v^2}{r}$
- explain what is meant by 'escape energy' and 'escape velocity'
- calculate the work done in moving a space vehicle from Earth to a place in space
- describe the forces acting and the resulting orbits of space probes that explore the solar system.

Glossary

Action and reaction Forces that occur together. They are equal and opposite. They act on two different objects.

Angular momentum The product of the object's moment of inertia, I, and its angular velocity, ω.

Centripetal acceleration The rate of change of velocity, directed towards the centre of a circle, of an object in circular motion.

Centripetal force The force that acts towards the centre of a circle and is responsible for an object changing direction.

Empirical Based on experimental evidence rather than deduced from theory.

Equilibrium A state when a mass has no unbalanced force acting upon it. All forces cancel.

Equipotential Places between which no energy need be transferred when a body moves between them.

Escape energy The energy transformed when moving from Earth's surface to infinity. An object given escape kinetic energy will continue to move away from Earth never to return.

Escape velocity The speed an object must attain in order to move unassisted to infinity. For Earth, a velocity of about 11 km s^{-1} is needed.

Free fall Moving under the action of gravity. Near Earth's surface this is an acceleration of 9.81 m s^{-2}.

Geostationary A satellite with a period of orbit of exactly 24 hours. Such satellites are located above Earth's Equator at a distance of about six Earth radii.

Gravitational field A place where there is a force on a mass. Near the surface of Earth the field is uniform and has a value of approximately 9.81 N kg^{-1}.

Gravity assist A technique for imparting extra kinetic energy to a space vehicle by using the gravitational attraction of a planet.

Impulse The product of a force and the time for which it acts.

Polar orbit A low Earth orbit, typically several hundred kilometres. Such satellites are used to observe Earth's surface activities.

Uniform gravitational field A place where the force on each kilogram is a constant value at all places in the field. The field near Earth's surface approximates to a uniform field.

Universal gravitation The attractive force that acts between all masses and is proportional to the product of their masses and inversely proportional to the square of their separation.

Vector A physical quantity that has both magnitude and direction. Vector quantities can easily be represented in diagrams by arrows.

Answers to Ready to Study test

R1

(a)

$$\text{Weight} = m \times g$$

$$= 0.5\,\text{kg} \times 9.81\,\text{ms}^{-2}$$

$$= 4.9\,\text{N}$$

(b) Mass = 0.5 kg

R2

Because of the shapes of the individual cornflakes, there is space between flakes when packed. There is therefore a lot of air in a full box and this reduces the density of the packet of cornflakes. They have the same mass as the sugar but the sugar is packed to a greater density.

R3

If we ignore air resistance, then each mass will be forced down vertically by a force = $m \times g$: their weight.

R4

(a) At the start the only force acting will be gravity and so the acceleration will be 9.81 m s^{-2} downwards.

(b) At this fast speed the air resistance is at its greatest. The resulting drag force balances the weight of a cornflake and so it continues to move with constant velocity under the action of two balanced forces – an equilibrium situation.

R5

The astronauts are in a state of free fall. They are falling towards Earth just as if they were free falling from an aeroplane. The spacecraft is also in free fall and so inside the craft the astronauts are not aware of the net gravitational force. Gravity is very much present, almost 9.81 N kg^{-1} in fact. The astronauts and their craft also happen to have a uniform sideways, orbiting, velocity. Their resulting motion is a curved path that just matches the curvature of Earth.

R6

You could have used the equation $a = \dfrac{v - u}{t}$ to work at the accelerations in (a)–(c).

(a)

$$a = \frac{40\,\text{ms}^{-1} - 20\,\text{ms}^{-1}}{1\,\text{s}}$$

$$= 20\,\text{ms}^{-2}$$

so the object will have positive acceleration of +20ms^{-2}.

(b)

$$a = \frac{-20\,\text{ms}^{-1} - 20\,\text{ms}^{-1}}{1\,\text{s}}$$

$$= -40\,\text{ms}^{-2}$$

so the object will have a negative acceleration of −40ms^{-2} (avoid the use of the term deceleration).

(c)

$$a = \frac{10\,\text{ms}^{-1} - 20\,\text{ms}^{-1}}{1\,\text{s}}$$

$$= -10\,\text{ms}^{-2}$$

so the object will have a negative acceleration of −10ms^{-2}.

(d) You may well find it impossible to give a value, but this particle is definitely accelerating since its direction has changed. Velocity is a vector quantity and any change in size or direction is a velocity change, i.e. an acceleration. A change requires a force to make it happen.

R7

The toy moves off in a straight path along a tangent to its original circular path. Since a force is needed to keep changing the direction of travel of the toy, when the force is removed the toy continues in uniform motion in a straight line.

Answers to questions in the text

Q1

(a)

Weight = mg

$\qquad$ = $0.5\,\text{kg} \times 1.6\,\text{m s}^{-2}$

$\qquad$ = $0.8\,\text{N}$

(b) It would accelerate down at $1.6\,\text{m s}^{-2}$.

Q2

(a)

Work done = force

$\qquad\qquad$ × distance moved by the force

$\qquad$ = $400\,\text{N} \times 6.0\,\text{m}$

$\qquad$ = $2400\,\text{J}$

$\qquad$ = $2.4 \times 10^3\,\text{J}$

$\qquad$ (to two significant figures)

(b)

Work done = mgh

$\qquad$ = $0.50\,\text{kg} \times 9.81\,\text{m s} \times 0.50\,\text{m}$

$\qquad$ = $2.5\,\text{J}$ (to two significant figures)

Q3

See Figure 4.27.

Q4

Units of impulse are N s. But force is defined as mass × acceleration (kg m s^{-2}). Hence the units N s become kg m s^{-2} s, or kg m s^{-1}.

Q5

(a)

Impulse = force × time

$\qquad$ = $150\,\text{N} \times 4\,\text{s}$

$\qquad$ = $600\,\text{N s}$

(b) Impulse equals change in momentum, so that is also $600\,\text{kg m s}^{-1}$.

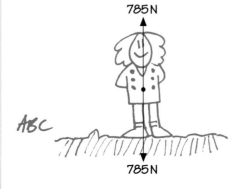

Figure 4.27
Answer to Question 3

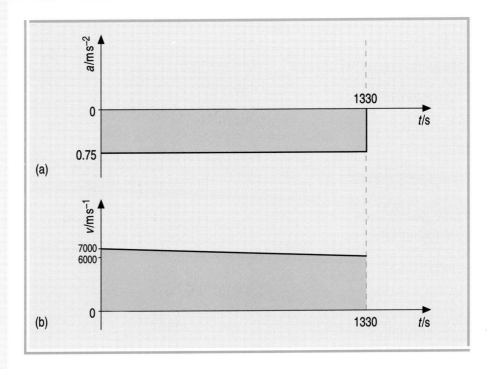

Figure 4.28
Answers to
Question 7

Q6

The momentum will change by 600 kg m s^{-1}, hence

$$\text{change in velocity} = \frac{\text{change in momentum}}{\text{mass}}$$

$$= \frac{600\,\text{kg m s}^{-1}}{250\,\text{kg}}$$

$$= 2.4\,\text{m s}^{-1}$$

So the impulse will change the velocity by 2.4 m s^{-1}, resulting in a final velocity of 2002.4 m s^{-1} or 1997.6 m s^{-1}.

Q7

(a) See Figure 4.28(a).

$$a = \frac{F}{m}$$

$$= \frac{300\,\text{N}}{400\,\text{kg}}$$

$$= 0.75\,\text{ms}^{-2}$$

(b) See Figure 4.28(b).

(c) The area 'under' the graph in Figure 4.28(a) represents the change in velocity.

Q8

(a)

$$\text{Force required} = \frac{0.20\,\text{kg} \times \left(4.0\,\text{ms}^{-1}\right)^2}{20\,\text{m}}$$

$$= 0.16\,\text{N}$$

This force is provided by the air lift acting on the bird's angled wings.

(b)

$$\text{Force required} = \frac{30\,\text{kg} \times \left(2.0\,\text{ms}^{-1}\right)^2}{2.0\,\text{m}}$$

$$= 60\,\text{N}$$

This force is provided by the tension in the child's arms and the friction beneath his/her feet.

(c)

$$\text{Force required} = \frac{6.0 \times 10^8 \, \text{kg} \times \left(21000 \, \text{ms}^{-1}\right)^2}{3.0 \times 10^{11} \, \text{m}}$$

$$= 882000 \, \text{N}$$

$$= 8.8 \times 10^5 \, \text{N}$$

(to two significant figures)

This force is provided by the gravitational attraction between the asteroid and the Sun.

Q9

(a) Io – just less than 2 days (1.8 days).

(b) Europa – about 3.5 days.

(c) Ganymede – just over 7 days (7.2 days).

(d) Callisto – about 17 days (16.7 days).

Q10

Io

$$\frac{r^3}{T^2} = \frac{\left(422000 \, \text{km}\right)^3}{\left(1.8 \, \text{d}\right)^2}$$

$$= 2.3 \times 10^{16} \, \text{km}^3 \text{d}^{-2}$$

Europa

$$\frac{r^3}{T^2} = \frac{\left(671000 \, \text{km}\right)^3}{\left(3.5 \, \text{d}\right)^2}$$

$$= 2.5 \times 10^{16} \, \text{km}^3 \text{d}^{-2}$$

Ganymede

$$\frac{r^3}{T^2} = \frac{\left(1070000 \, \text{km}\right)^3}{\left(7.2 \, \text{d}\right)^2}$$

$$= 2.4 \times 10^{16} \, \text{km}^3 \text{d}^{-2}$$

Callisto

$$\frac{r^3}{T^2} = \frac{\left(1880000 \, \text{km}\right)^3}{\left(17 \, \text{d}\right)^2}$$

$$= 2.3 \times 10^{16} \, \text{km}^3 \text{d}^{-2}$$

Mean value $= 2.4 \times 10^{16} \, \text{km}^3 \, \text{d}^{-2}$

(to two significant figures)

Q11

As

$$\frac{r^3}{T^2} = 2.4 \times 10^{16} \, \text{km}^3 \, \text{d}^{-2}$$

$$T^2 = \frac{\left(11.5 \times 10^6 \, \text{km}\right)^3}{2.4 \times 10^{16} \, \text{km}^3 \, \text{d}^{-2}}$$

$$= 6.337 \times 10^4 \, \text{d}^2$$

then $T = 250$ days (to two significant figures)

Q12

Here is one example of each; there are plenty of others.

(a) Facts, e.g. the objects are about 2–4 km across.

(b) Predictions, e.g. circular travelling waves will be produced on impact.

(c) Technology, e.g. the computer simulation by the nCube 2 computer.

Q13

You may have listed those shown in Table 4.1; there are more.

Table 4.1 Answer to Question 13

Information	Guardian	Daily Telegraph
Existence of extra terrestrial agency	✔	
Siberian comet impact	✔	
Comet impact more frequent than people realize (every 300 years)	✔	
Scientists immoral because they don't warn the public of the dangers	✔	
Dinosaurs may have been destroyed by a comet 25 million years ago	✔	✔

Q14

If the public become interested these events then politicians are more likely to support funding for scientific research.

The public should be informed about comets because they present dangers to life on Earth and politicians must act on the public's behalf.

Studying the sky can 'give perspective to our everyday lives'.

Q15

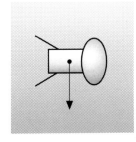

(a) See Figure 4.29.

Figure 4.29
Answer to Question 15(a)

(b) They are in a state of free fall.

(c) (i) If momentum is given to a mass of gas in one direction then this must be accompanied by an equal momentum in the reverse direction.

(ii)

$$\text{Impulse} = F \times t$$
$$= 400\,\text{N} \times 8.0\,\text{s}$$
$$= 3200\,\text{N s}$$

(iii) A second impulse would be needed to stop the space probe from rotating for ever.

Q16

(a)

$$\text{Force on P} = \frac{GM \times 2000\,\text{kg}}{\left(2.0 \times 10^8\,\text{km}\right)^2}$$
$$= GM \times 5.0 \times 10^{-14}\,\text{N}$$

$$\text{Force on Q} = \frac{GM \times 4000\,\text{kg}}{\left(4.0 \times 10^8\,\text{km}\right)^2}$$
$$= GM \times 2.5 \times 10^{-14}\,\text{N}$$

(b) As P will be subjected to a stronger field it will move ahead and so the PQ distance will increase. The distance PQ will increase until P crashes into the surface.

(c) (i) The gravitational field strength at a point is given by the size and direction of the force on a unit mass placed at that point.

(ii) The curve is a $1/r^2$ shape.

(iii) Calculate the area under the curve between these places.

Q17

(a) The gravitational attraction between Titan and Saturn acts at right angles to Titan's motion. It therefore provides a centripetal force.

(b) (i) 16 days.

(ii) About 1 500 000 km

(iii)

$$v = \frac{2\pi r}{T}$$

$$= \frac{2\pi \times 1.5 \times 10^9 \, \text{m}}{16 \times 24 \times 3600 \, \text{s}}$$

$$= 6.8 \times 10^3 \, \text{ms}^{-1} \text{ (to two significant figures)}$$

(iv)

$$a = \frac{v^2}{r}$$

$$= \frac{\left(6.8 \times 10^3 \, \text{ms}^{-1}\right)^2}{1.5 \times 10^9 \, \text{m}}$$

$$= 0.03 \, \text{ms}^{-2} \text{ (to two significant figures)}$$

(c)

$$M = \frac{r^3}{T^2} \frac{4\pi^2}{G}$$

$$= \frac{\left(1.5 \times 10^9 \, \text{m}\right)^3}{\left(16 \times 24 \times 3600 \, \text{s}\right)^2} \times \frac{4\pi^2}{6.7 \times 10^{-11} \, \text{Nm}^2 \, \text{kg}^{-2}}$$

$$= 1.04061 \times 10^{27} \, \text{kg}$$

$$= 1.0 \, \text{kg} \text{ (to two significant figures)}$$

Q18

(a)

$$a = \frac{9.81 \, \text{ms}^{-2}}{(60)^2}$$

$$= 0.0027 \, \text{ms}^{-2}$$

(b) It is also moving with a constant tangential velocity. Its motion is therefore a circle that just manages to keep falling to Earth at the same rate as Earth's surface curves.

(c) The statement is not true; there is some gravity at the surface of the Moon (about one-sixth of that on Earth) and atmosphere does not cause gravity. The lack of atmosphere on the Moon can be attributed to the fact that its gravity was not strong enough to hold gas particles down on to the surface.

Appendix 4.1
Angular momentum

Particles in orbit

The linear momentum of a moving particle is simply the product of its mass and velocity. It is conserved in all interactions

$$\text{momentum, } p = mv$$

When a particle moves in a circle, as does the mass swung around by an Olympic hammer thrower or an electron orbiting the nucleus of an atom, it has a greater turning effect the greater its radius of orbit. For a given rate of revolution, the greater the radius of orbit the faster the object or particle must move. The rate of revolution is called the angular velocity, ω. It is related to the actual velocity of the object by

$$\omega = \frac{v}{r} \text{ or } v = r\omega$$

For two masses orbiting with the same angular velocity but at different radii, the one at the greater radius will move faster, have the greater linear momentum, mv, and have a greater angular momentum, often called the moment of momentum and calculated from

$$\text{angular momentum} = mv \times r$$

or

$$\text{angular momentum} = mr^2\omega$$

Spinning masses

When a solid object spins about an axis at a steady rate, the rate of spin is its angular velocity, ω. A planet that spins once in 24 days has an angular velocity of 360° in 24 days or 15° per day. Measured in radians this is a rate

of $\dfrac{2\pi \text{ radians}}{24 \text{ days}}$ or $\dfrac{\pi}{12}$ radians per day.

Every part of the planet will have this angular velocity even though those parts near the centre will be moving more slowly than the parts near the planet's surface.

The total angular momentum of a complex spinning body is just the sum of the angular momentum of all of the parts of the body.

Total angular momentum

$$= \text{sum of} \left[m_1 r_1^2 \omega + m_2 r_2^2 \omega + ... \right]$$

$$= \left(\text{sum of all } mr^2 \text{ products} \right)\omega$$

$$= I\omega$$

I is called the moment of inertia of the spinning body. It is the sum of all the mr^2 parts of a body. If a body has most of its mass distributed near the axis of spin then I will be small. A body with much of its mass situated at greater radii will have a larger value for I. Such a mass will be difficult to start to spin but equally difficult to stop spinning. It will have considerable angular momentum simply through the distribution of its mass. A flywheel is designed to keep a machine rotating steadily. The mass of a flywheel is concentrated around its outer rim giving it a large moment of inertia and a large angular momentum. Of the two spinning satellites in Figure 4.30, B has the greater angular momentum.

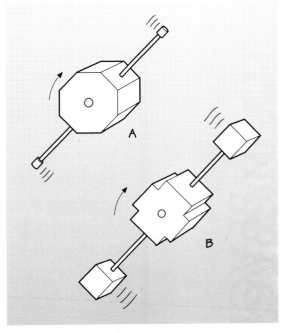

Figure 4.30 Spinning satellites

Although we have placed a man on the Moon and have landed a probe on Mars the information gained by such adventures is but a drop in the ocean compared with the information we gain from simply looking into space. Naked eyes, cameras and telescopes have enabled us to make predictions about events such as eclipses and to chart the sky for purposes of navigation, time-keeping and mythology. It is by collecting and analysing the light from space that we have built up virtually our entire picture of the Universe. Telescope design has been an important factor in this search to understand the heavens. In this section we look at light and optical instruments, and in particular at the problems that arise when trying to secure a crisp, clear and sharp image of an object that may be a million light years away.

READY TO STUDY TEST

Before you begin this section you should be able to:

- understand that we see objects from the light they reflect or emit
- describe how a spectrum of colours can be produced from white light
- name some radiations that are detectable beyond the visible spectrum
- describe the wave properties of light and explain the terms 'amplitude', 'wavelength' and 'frequency'
- state the speed at which waves in the electromagnetic spectrum travel in a vacuum
- explain that light is a transverse wave and that for all waves velocity = frequency × wavelength, $v = f \times \lambda$
- describe how transverse waves can combine to produce constructive and destructive interference (see page 88 of the SLIPP unit *Physics, Jazz and Pop*)
- describe examples of reflection and refraction of light that occur in everyday life.

QUESTIONS

R1 Explain why a red T-shirt appears red in sunlight.

R2 The red T-shirt worn in a disco lit with blue lights appears black. Why?

R3 What do ultraviolet and microwave radiations have in common?

LIGHT IN SPACE

R4   When you look into a shop window you can often see your own reflection as well as the items in the window display. How does the passage of light explain both these observations.

R5   Light is a transverse wave. Draw a diagram to explain what is meant by 'transverse'.

R6   The speed of radio waves is 3.0×10^8 m s^{-1}.

(a) Calculate the frequency of radio waves with wavelength 1500 m

(b) Calculate the wavelength of the waves from a radio station broadcasting at a frequency of 95.8×10^6 Hz.

R7   Sketch a displacement versus time graph for the resultant wave produced when two waves with the same amplitude and phase meet.

5.1 Twinkle twinkle little star, how I wonder what you are …

Everyone notices that stars twinkle, but why do they? The twinkle we see is a feature of the passage of light through Earth's atmosphere. This happens just at the end of the light's journey through space. A journey that may have taken several hundred years in a straight line only to be deflected by the turbulence in Earth's atmosphere in the last millisecond of the journey. The fact that the path is deflected by Earth's turbulent atmosphere is due to **refraction**. As the light passes through layers of atmosphere of different densities and temperatures so it changes speed and direction. The atmosphere presents the light with a medium of varying **refractive index**. This is illustrated in Figure 5.1 overleaf.

Why are many of the world's modern observatories built high upon mountains, for example Mount Palomar in California and Mauna Kea in Hawaii? What additional advantages does such a location offer to the astronomer?

They place the telescopes on mountains so that they are above much of the warm, polluted atmosphere. Such heights are also above low-lying cloud and away from city light pollution.

twinkle twinkle little star...

atmosphere

Figure 5.1
Refraction of light by
Earth's atmosphere

The refractive index of a material is related to the speed at which light travels through it. It is defined by:

$$\text{refractive index} = \frac{\text{speed of light through a vacuum}}{\text{speed of light through the material}}$$

$$n = \frac{c_{vac}}{c_{medium}}$$

Refractive indices are always greater than 1 as light travels at its greatest speed through a vacuum (space for our purposes) at about 3.0×10^8 m s^{-1}. Some typical values of n are shown in Table 5.1. (*Note:* Crown and flint are types of glass with minerals combined in different proportions.)

Table 5.1 Refractive indices of various materials

Material	Refractive index
Vacuum	1
Air	1.0003
Water	1.33
Crown glass	1.51
Flint glass	1.65

Q1 Use the data in Table 5.1 to calculate the speed of light through water. ◆

Q2 Through which type of glass would light be slowed down most? ◆

Makers of optical instruments need to know the refractive index of each type of material they use. Compound lenses made from two or more types of glass of different refractive indices will produce clearer images. Given a piece of transparent material you can calculate its refractive index following a series of measurements, as the following exploration shows.

Exploration 5.1
Determining the refractive index of a transparent material

Apparatus:

◆ raybox ◆ power supply ◆ transparent block (glass or Perspex)
◆ sheet of white paper ◆ protractor

40-45
MINUTES

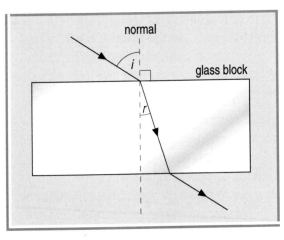

In a darkened room with a raybox and a glass or Perspex block it is relatively easy to determine the refractive index of a material and hence calculate the speed of light through the material. Trace the path of a ray through the medium as shown in Figure 5.2.

Construct a 90° 'normal' line and measure i and r values up to this line. Repeat your measurements and calculations for various values of i.

Figure 5.2 The path of a ray through a glass block

The angles i and r need to be measured using the protractor. The refractive index of the medium is found from the ratio $\dfrac{\sin i}{\sin r}$. This relationship, $n = \dfrac{\sin i}{\sin r}$, is known as **Snel's law**.

In this simple determination we have assumed that the speed of light through air is the same as that for a vacuum, i.e. the refractive index of air is 1. From Table 5.1 is this a reasonable assumption?

Yes, look at Table 5.1 to compare their refractive indices.

More generally, if light passes from a medium of refractive index n_1 to one with index n_2, Snel's law would become

$n_1 \sin i = n_2 \sin r$

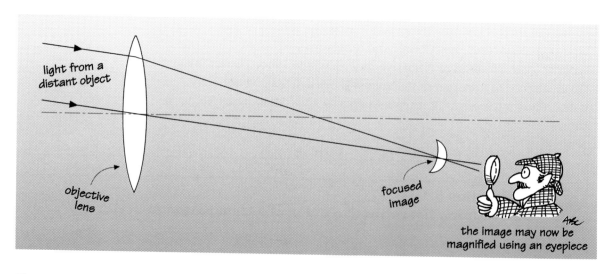

light from a distant object

objective lens

focused image

the image may now be magnified using an eyepiece

Figure 5.3
A simplified diagram of a refracting telescope

The first telescopes to be built used the refracting properties of glass to change the path of starlight. In a refracting telescope an **objective lens** focuses the light from a distant object at a point (see Figure 5.3). The distance of this point from the lens is called the **focal length**. A **real image** of the distant object is located at this point and can be captured on a sheet of paper or on photographic film. If desired, the image can be magnified by a second lens, called the telescope eyepiece.

One of the main problems encountered by early telescope makers was that of **chromatic aberration** (literally colour errors). Light of different wavelengths, red and blue for example, are deviated by different amounts as they pass through glass. This is most easily seen using a raybox and a prism. In Figure 5.4(a) you will notice that blue light is deviated more than red light. This means that the refractive index of glass must vary with the wavelength of the light. The degree of variation depends on the type of glass. Table 5.2 shows the extent of this variation.

Table 5.2 Variation of refractive index between red and blue light

Refractive index	Red light	Blue light
n (crown glass)	1.515	1.532
n (flint glass)	1.644	1.685

A single lens will focus red light at a different point compared with blue light producing chromatic aberrations. This means a bright white star image will have red/blue edges. Chromatic aberration is particularly evident when using budget-priced binoculars and telescopes.

A solution to the problem of chromatic aberration is to combine two lenses, one made from flint glass the other from crown glass. Such a combination is called an **achromatic lens** and it virtually eliminates chromatic aberration. It is possible to create a triple glass objective lens called an apochromatic lens. This produces the highest quality image but it can double the price of your telescope.

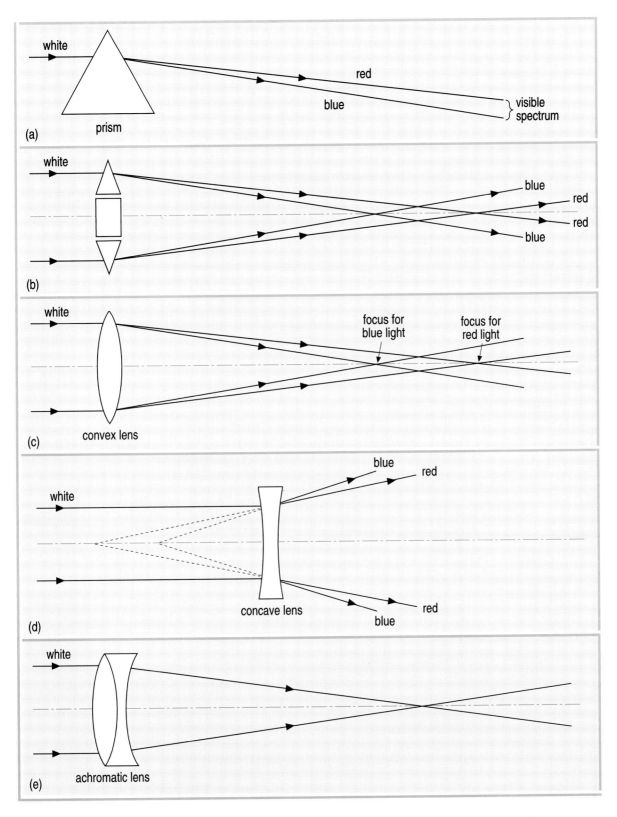

Figure 5.4 (a) Deviation of red and blue light by a prism; (b) a single lens acting as two prisms to show effect of chromatic aberration; (c) a single convex lens producing chromatic aberration; (d) a single concave lens producing chromatic aberration; (e) an achromatic lens producing a single focal point for white light

An achromatic lens system, as in Figure 5.4(e), uses two lenses glued together. How do the lenses differ?

They are made from glass of different refractive indices and one is a concave lens and the other a convex lens.

 Exploration 5.2   Chromatic aberration

Apparatus:

◆ 12 V/24 W vertical filament lamp and holder ◆ 12 V power supply ◆ 12.5 cm or 10 cm convex lens and holder ◆ two plastic filters each about 10 cm square (one blue, one red) ◆ piece of card to cut out with scissors and use as a lens stop

Set up a simple optical system as shown in Figure 5.5. The lamp is best shielded to prevent stray light. Ensure that the filament lines up with the central axis through the lens.

lamp positioned at prime focus position of lens

magnified image of filament

Figure 5.5
Apparatus for
Exploration 5.2

By placing the lamp close to the **prime focus** of the lens you will obtain a sharp, magnified image of the filament on a screen at the far end of the bench. A little adjustment of lamp and screen will give a sharp image. The screen can be as far away as you like. Try projecting a sharp image across the room (you will need a very dark room).

Now place a blue and then a red filter in front of the lens in turn. For each filter note the changes seen at the image. Find the position of the sharpest image of the lamp filament. You should find that each filter creates its own sharpest image distance.

Note down these positions and measure the two lamp-to-image distances.

What can you deduce about the effect that wavelength has on image position?

Try to eliminate the chromatic effect by masking off the outer edge of the lens. This is called stopping down the lens. The image will be fainter but is there as much chromatic aberration?

Finally a word about an optical problem that can arise in lens systems. When light passes through a lens it crosses two interfaces. From air to glass as it enters and then from glass to air as it leaves. At each interface a small fraction of the light is reflected (see Figure 5.6a). The second reflection is perhaps unexpected as the light is travelling from glass to air. This is called an internal reflection. If the angle at which the light strikes this second interface is larger than a critical value all the light will be internally reflected – a situation known as **total internal reflection**.

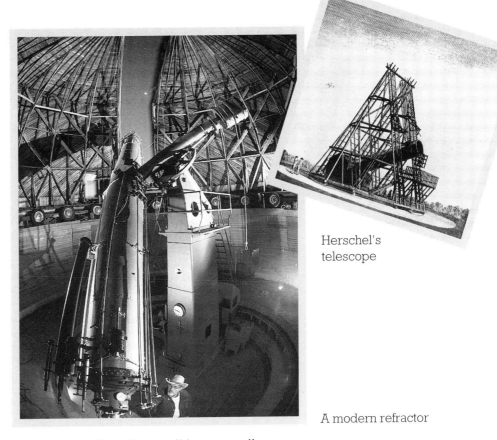

Herschel's telescope

A modern refractor

 Why is this a problem?

Less energy is transmitted, which gives a dimmer image, so any details are harder to see.

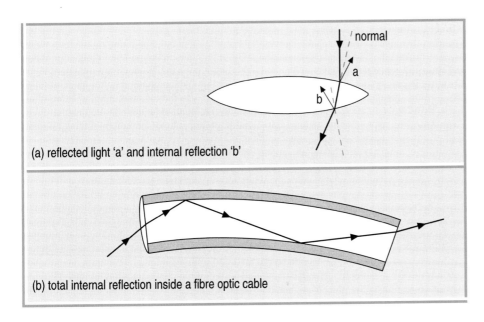

(a) reflected light 'a' and internal reflection 'b'

(b) total internal reflection inside a fibre optic cable

Figure 5.6
(a) Reflections as light passes through a lens; (b) total internal reflection

In telescope lenses total internal reflection does not occur as the angle of incidence is below the **critical angle**. However, in a fibre optic cable the incident angle is designed to be greater than the critical angle and the total internal reflections ensure that the light remains within the cable. For light travelling from a dense medium like glass of refractive index n into air, the critical angle, c, can be calculated as from

$$\sin c = \frac{1}{n}$$

Q3   If the refractive index of a thin optical fibre is 1.55, calculate the critical angle that would ensure total internal reflection. ◆

E ◆ **Exploration 5.3   Finding a critical angle**

Apparatus:

◆ raybox ◆ power supply ◆ semicircular block
◆ sheet of white paper

30 MINUTES

Set up the curved transparent block and raybox in the position shown in Figure 5.7. Place the paper beneath the block and mark in pencil the outline shape of the block and also a point along the

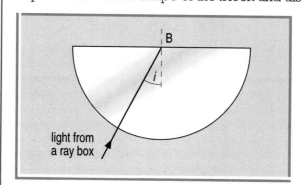

flat edge, B. Construct a line at right angles to the flat edge passing through B.

Your angles will be measured from this line, called a 'normal'.

Figure 5.7   The arrangement for Exploration 5.3

Direct a single ray of light towards point B from within the block. Vary the angle of incidence, i, and observe what happens to the direction of the emerging ray. At one particular value of incident angle you will detect the emerging beam running parallel to the flat edge of the block. A fractional increase in the value of angle i will cause total internal reflection. At this critical point, mark and measure i. This is the critical angle for your block/air interface.

If you calculated a value for the refractive index of a transparent material for Exploration 5.1, use the equation $\sin c = \dfrac{1}{n}$ to calculate a value for the critical angle. Compare this to the angle you have just measured.

5.2 Reflecting telescopes

Light from a distant object can just as easily be brought to a **focal point** by a curved mirror as by a lens. A mirror is cheaper to make as the type of glass used is less critical. What is important is the quality of finish on the mirror surface. Both the precise shape and the reflective coating will influence the image quality. Some early reflectors used metal mirrors. One advantage of a mirror is that it needs only one finished surface. A further advantage of a mirror is its location. Telescopes directed towards the heavens will have their mirrors at their base. This makes guiding and supporting the weight of a large mirror much more manageable.

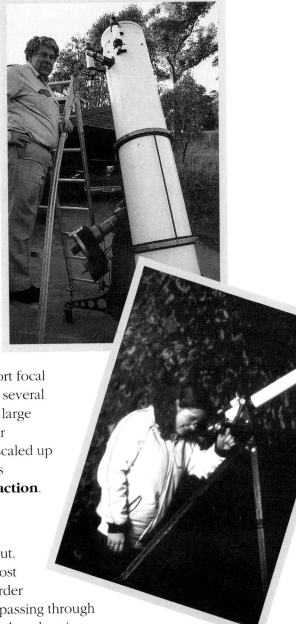

A 300 mm reflecting telescope

One advantage of the simpler design of a mirror is that mirrors can be made much wider than lenses. The **apertures**, or diameters, of reflecting telescopes range typically from 110 mm for a beginners' instrument to over 5.0 m on an international research instrument. The sheer size of these apertures gives one major advantage to reflecting telescopes – they can see dimmer, and therefore more distant, objects. It is often the case that amateur astronomers use the superior light gathering power of a 300 mm aperture reflector to look at faint galaxies but will turn to their smaller aperture 80 mm refractors for better image quality when looking at details of something brighter – the rings of Saturn, for example.

Q4 The light gathering power of any lens or mirror depends on its surface area. What would be the difference in light gathering power between a circular lens of diameter 75 mm and a circular mirror of diameter 300 mm? ◆

Radio telescopes are often curved reflectors with very short focal lengths. Their apertures can range from several metres to several hundred metres. Radio signals from space are weak, so a large aperture is needed. Also, radio waves have a much longer wavelength than visible light, so everything needs to be scaled up accordingly. The longer wavelength of radio waves poses astronomers with an additional problem caused by **diffraction**.

The problem of diffraction

When waves pass through an aperture they will spread out. This is called diffraction. It happens to all waves but is most noticeable when the size of the aperture is of the same order (about the same size) as the wavelength of the radiation passing through it. To reduce the effect of diffraction, the aperture-to-wavelength ratio should be made as large as possible.

An 80 mm refractor

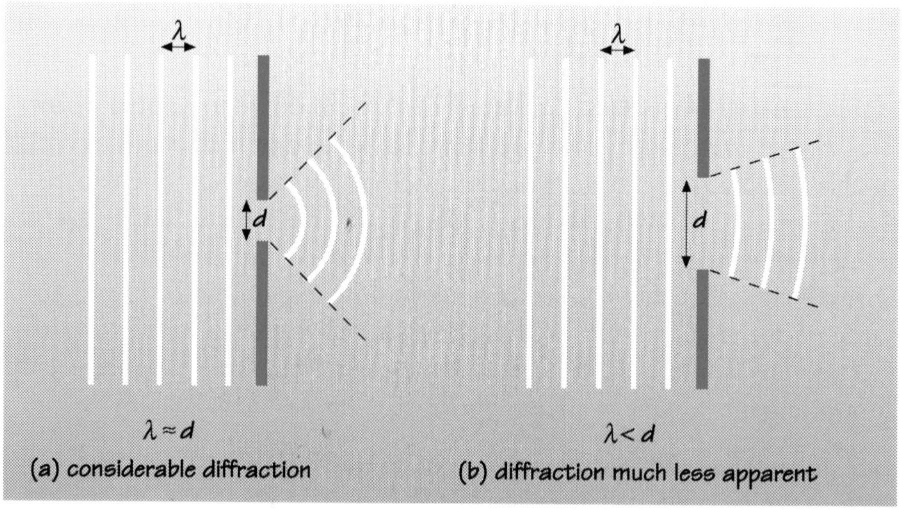

Figure 5.8
(a) Diffraction
through a small
aperture;
(b) reduced
diffraction through
a larger aperture

From Figure 5.8 you can see how the angular spread is altered by the size
of the aperture.

> If the wavelength of the light changes to a smaller wavelength, what
> happens to the aperture-to-wavelength ratio? How will this change
> the diffraction?

The aperture-to-wavelength ratio increases so the diffraction
decreases and the light spreads less for both apertures.

For visible light, larger aperture telescopes will minimize diffraction. This
is another advantage of a large aperture. The problem of diffraction
results in a spreading of the light in the focused image. For circular
apertures the spread takes the shape of fuzzy diffraction rings. No
amount of careful focusing will reduce this effect. It is simply a property
of waves.

In Exploration 5.4 you can demonstrate the effect of diffraction using
microwaves and a laser.

Exploration 5.4 Demonstrating diffraction using a microwave source and/or a laser

Part (i) Using microwaves

Apparatus:

- a microwave transmitter, about 10 GHz ◆ receiver
- some metal screens

Set up the transmitter behind two metal screens separated by about 10 cm as shown in Figure 5.9(a). Place your microwave detector to one side so that it receives little or no signal. Now close the gap slowly by pushing the metal screens together. You should notice that the detector signal increases even though the gap allowing microwaves through is closing.

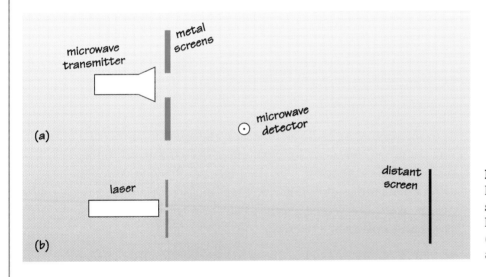

Figure 5.9 Experimental set-up for Exploration 5.4 (viewed from above)

Part (ii) Using visible laser light

Apparatus:

- laser ◆ narrow slit

In a dark room set up the laser behind a single mounted slit as shown in Figure 5.9(b). Look at a screen a few metres away. You will notice that the vertical slit will produce a horizontal diffraction effect. Now replace the single slit with a single circular aperture and look again at the diffraction pattern. You may be able to use a slit of variable width or holes of different diameters.

When waves pass through an aperture, the diffraction effect produces a particular pattern. This is of a broad central spread accompanied by fainter fringes beyond the central spread. You may have noticed this pattern when doing Exploration 5.4. For waves of wavelength λ, passing through an aperture of diameter d, the central angular spread caused by diffraction is of the order of $\dfrac{\lambda}{d}$ radians.

For a 300 mm diameter reflecting telescope operating at visible wavelengths of 5.0×10^{-7} m this angle can be calculated as about

$$\frac{\lambda}{d} = \frac{5.0 \times 10^{-7}\,\text{m}}{300 \times 10^{-3}\,\text{m}}$$

$$= 1.7 \times 10^{-6}\,\text{radians}$$

However, for a 12 m radio dish operating at 1.0 m wavelength the angle becomes

$$\frac{\lambda}{d} = \frac{1.0\,\text{m}}{12\,\text{m}}$$

$$= 0.08\,\text{radians}$$

You can see that for radio astronomers the angular spread of a diffraction ring pattern is considerable. What effect does this have on the performance of the telescope? The biggest diffraction issue for astronomers is the effect it has on their ability to distinguish two or more nearby objects. This is called the ability to resolve objects or the **resolving power** of a telescope.

So, the resolution of a telescope is the smallest angular separation at which two objects can be distinguished by the observer as separate. If an instrument has a resolving power of 2.0×10^{-5} radians then two nearby stars separated by an angle of 4.0×10^{-5} radians will be seen as separate.

An approximate way to calculate the resolving power of a telescope is to divide the wavelength of the radiation by the telescope aperture

$$\text{resolving power} = \frac{\text{wavelength}}{\text{aperture}}$$

Exploration 5.5   Resolving power of optical systems

30 MINUTES

Apparatus:

- pair of binoculars or the school or college telescope   ◆   a fine pencil
- sheet of white paper

> Never look at the Sun through an optical instrument.

Use a fine pencil to draw two lines, about 1 mm apart, on a sheet of white paper. We will call this distance 's'. Pin the sheet on a wall and look at the two lines as you move back away from them. Measure the distance, D, from the paper to your eyes at which you just can no longer distinguish them as two separate lines. This is the limit of your ability to resolve the lines. Repeat this using binoculars and/or a telescope. You may need to use a long corridor or the playing field for the telescope observation.

For each observation calculate the angle created by the two lines and the centre of your observing instrument, i.e. s/D at the resolving limit. This angle, in radians, is the resolving power of your optical system.

Decide which of these observations could be achieved with your instruments:

- resolving two planetary rings, separated by 1.5×10^{-4} radians
- resolving Alcor and Mizar, an optical binary system, separated by 4.0×10^{-3} radians.

Apart from building larger aperture telescopes, the only option left to astronomers who want to improve their resolution is to select shorter wavelength radiation. Diffraction effects reduce with shorter wavelengths, so by using a blue filter an astronomer using visible radiation can improve resolving power (at the loss of brightness, it must be added).

For the radio astronomer there is not always the option of selecting shorter wavelength radiation – the aerials of radio receivers are designed to detect a particular wavelength. Information from interstellar hydrogen, for example, is at a wavelength of 21 cm. However, there is one ingenious solution to improve resolution and it uses the very wave nature of light that causes the problem in the first place.

Interferometry

When two waves are added together their amplitudes either add constructively or subtract destructively to produce a resultant **interference pattern**. (Further details of **constructive** and **destructive** **interference** can be found in the SLIPP unit *Physics, Jazz and Pop*, pages 87–8.)

If the signals received by two radio telescopes are added they will also produce their own interference pattern – this is the principle behind the **interferometer** (see Figure 5.10). It is based upon the fact that the signals arriving at the two dishes will be slightly out of **phase** and so the diffraction rings will all but cancel out. The resulting resolution when two

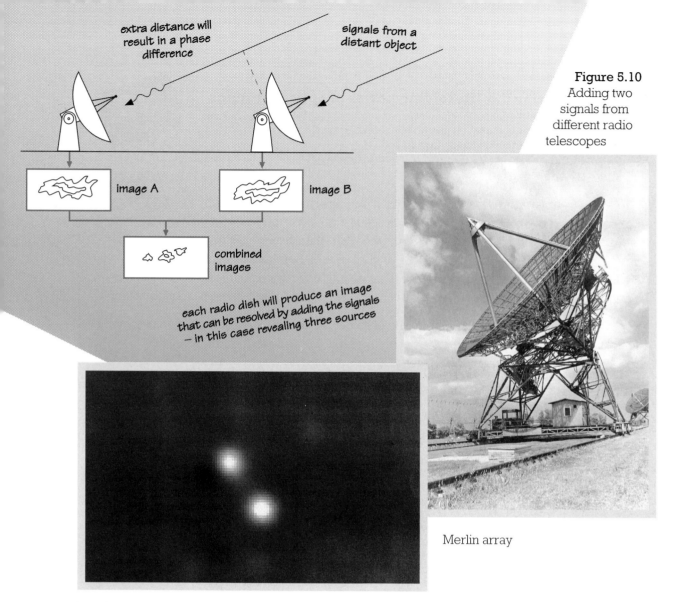

Figure 5.10
Adding two signals from different radio telescopes

extra distance will result in a phase difference

signals from a distant object

image A

image B

combined images

each radio dish will produce an image that can be resolved by adding the signals — in this case revealing three sources

Merlin array

Interferometer image of Capella

telescopes are combined in this way is as good as that from a single telescope with an aperture the size of the separation of the two telescopes being combined. So two telescopes 100 m apart will have the resolution of a single 100 m diameter dish.

Computer technology can now add the signals from a string of small radio telescopes, called a Very Large Array (VLA) and produce a sharp radio image with much improved resolution. One such VLA is the Merlin array in Cambridge.

It is now possible to link up two received signals from telescopes separated by continents, thereby improving resolution to that equivalent to a single dish thousands of kilometres in diameter. Such a telescope is known as a Very Long Baseline Interferometer (VLBI).

The interferometer technique has recently been adapted for improving the resolution of optical telescopes at the University of Cambridge. The Cambridge Optical Aperture Synthesis Telescope (COAST), combined the light from four 40 cm mirrors to produce an interferometer image of the bright star Capella. As the mirrors are about 7 m apart, the resulting interferometer has the resolving power of a single 7 m mirror. The image is so sharp that it manages to resolve Capella into two optical components, the first time astronomers have ever seen the two components. (See the Further Reading and Resources section for information on COAST on the Internet.)

40 MINUTES

E **Exploration 5.6 Observing interference patterns**

Observe safety rules when using a laser. Never point it at anyone, never look into the beam and place a warning notice on the door of the room.

Apparatus:

◆ laser ◆ double slit in a suitable holder

A laser and a double slit can be used to demonstrate the interference of two sources of light.

Place the double slit close to the laser and in a darkened room observe the pattern on a distant screen about two or three metres away. Figure 5.11 shows the position of the first diffraction image.

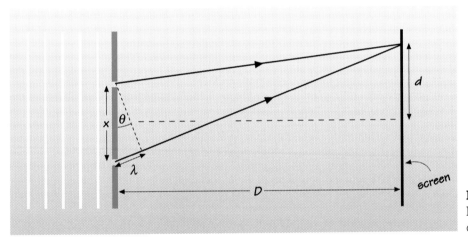

Figure 5.11 Position of first diffraction image

λ is the extra distance taken by waves passing through the bottom slit. If this extra distance is exactly one wavelength then, for small values of θ

$$\sin \theta = \theta$$
$$= \frac{\lambda}{x} \tag{5.1}$$

By measuring the distance D between the slit and the image, and the position of the first image, d, then for small values of θ

$$\theta = \frac{d}{D} \tag{5.2}$$

combining Equations (5.1) and (5.2) gives

$$\frac{\lambda}{x} = \frac{d}{D}$$

and

$$\text{resolving power (or resolution)} = \frac{x}{D}$$

$$= \frac{\lambda}{d}$$

If you use a magnifying glass or slide projector technique to determine the slit separation, x, you can use this relationship to find a value for the wavelength of the laser light you used.

Q5 Calculate the resolution of a radio interferometer operating at a wavelength of 21 cm if the baseline between its dishes is 10 000 km. How does this compare with the resolution from a small amateur optical telescope? ◆

Q6 The star Castor is in fact a double star whose two components are separated by only 2.0×10^{-5} radians. If the wavelength of the light they emit is 5.0×10^{-7} m, calculate the minimum aperture telescope that would be able to resolve the two components. ◆

5.3 Electronic imaging

Light from distant stars and galaxies can be very feeble indeed by the time it reaches Earth and passes along your telescope tube to your eye. To allow time for such feeble light to be captured, astronomers photograph the sky capturing light over a period of many minutes or hours. Photographic film allows the steady build up of a chemical reaction over time to create more and more dense images. By transferring the energy in single photons of light to kinetic energy of photoelectrons it is now possible to register the arrival of a single photon electronically.

This is achieved with a **CCD (Charge Coupled Device)** camera. Charge Coupled Devices are now available for amateur use. When a photon strikes an electron in a crystal of **p-type silicon**, it frees the electron, which is attracted to a positively charged collector. A typical design is to locate a 512×512 array of collectors, called **pixels**, in an imaging area about 8 mm × 8 mm. Each pixel, about 15×10^{-6} m square, accumulates captured photoelectrons. The number of electrons will determine the brightness of the image at that pixel location.

CCD images are sensitive to background thermal noise and so need to be cooled when used, to about 30°C below ambient (room) temperature. ('Noise' is a scientific term used to describe unwanted information, in this case it would be electrons produced during the CCD operation but not from the light from the object in question. One source of noise would be cosmic rays, which arrive randomly from space and would liberate unwanted photoelectrons.) The electronic image produced by a CCD can be downloaded on to a computer disk, processed to eliminate noise and displayed at will.

5.4 Looking back in time

In one second the light from a hand flashlight could travel into space on a dark night to a distance of about seven times around Earth, roughly the distance to the Moon. This is a distance of one **light second**. Travelling at this speed for eight minutes will take us to the Sun. To move to Saturn at this speed would take about an hour and a half. The star nearest to our solar system, Proxima Centauri, is just over four **light years** away.

This means that should we catch a glimpse of Proxima Centauri one dark night we would have captured light that had left the star over four years ago. We would be looking at what had occurred four years ago. In this sense looking into space is looking into the past. Many of the stars you see on a dark night will be hundreds of light years away. When you see these stars you are indeed looking back hundreds of years into the history of the Universe.

The Andromeda nebula, one of our nearby neighbouring galaxies, is about 200 million light years away. It can just be seen with the naked eye – looking back 200 million years into history. Estimates of the age of the Universe vary but are currently between 13 and 17 Gyr ($13–17 \times 10^9$ yr).

The bright star Betelgeuse is about 650 light years away. You might easily capture some light from Betelgeuse tonight if it is a clear night. Name four important historical events that have occurred since this light left Betelgeuse.

Any four of your choosing from before Tudor times to the present day: great wars, great people, inventions, your birth, etc.

Information beyond the visible spectrum

We have already made a reference to the 21 cm radio wavelength information from hydrogen gas in space. The breadth of radiations that celestial objects emit is as broad as the electromagnetic spectrum itself. This has led to the development of X-ray telescopes, infrared telescopes, ultraviolet telescopes, and so on.

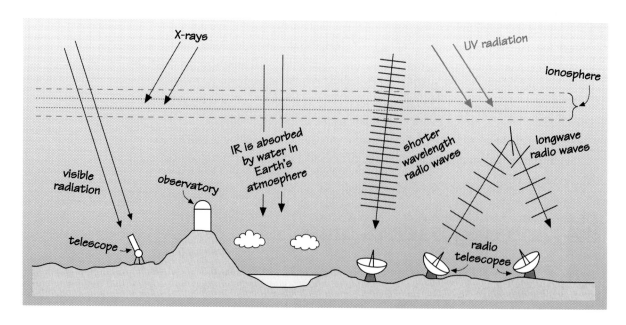

Figure 5.12
Radiation from space reaching Earth

However, the atmosphere poses the greatest challenge when observing at any single wavelength. We started this section with the twinkle twinkle little star rhyme – a reference to one way in which the atmosphere influences light. We shall end by looking at the other interactions between radiation and the atmosphere. Figure 5.12 summarizes the situation across the electromagnetic spectrum.

Clouds and atmospheric pollution are the main obstacles to astronomers making observations in visible light. For radio astronomers there are some shortwave bands that manage to pass through the atmosphere and, of course, these can penetrate clouds and are detectable during day and night. Life in the world of radio astronomy is not limited to dark clear night skies. As for infrared, X-ray and ultraviolet astronomers, theirs is not an easy lot. Their telescopes must be placed above Earth's atmosphere. The advent of satellite launching systems using rockets and the Space Shuttles has allowed such telescopes to be located in Earth orbit and these offer images of stars, planets and galaxies across the full range of the electromagnetic spectrum.

5.5 Public science – space telescopes

Since you cannot actually carry out experiments on astronomical objects, most of astronomy is concerned with collecting radiation – from gamma-rays to radio waves – from stars and galaxies. And to reach out into the depths of space, you need ever larger telescopes, with ever more sensitive equipment. One problem facing astronomy is that the air which is so vital for keeping us alive cuts out many wavelength regions, such as ultraviolet radiation, and introduces distortions into those it lets through.

One technique to improve sensitivity is to put your telescope above Earth's atmosphere. The most ambitious of such space observatories is the Hubble Space Telescope, placed in an orbit low enough that it can be reached by the Space Shuttle so that its instruments can regularly be updated, but high enough to be free of our troublesome atmosphere. The project to design and build the telescope and put it into orbit cost billions of dollars.

But, in 1990, soon after it was launched from the Shuttle, Hubble was found to be seriously flawed. The main telescope mirror had been polished to the wrong focal length; all the pictures were fuzzy, no better than could be obtained by a small telescope back down on the ground. Although computer programmers worked out ingenious ways of getting round this problem, it was not until a second Shuttle mission in 1993 fitted Hubble with a set of corrective 'spectacles' that the real power of the telescope was revealed.

Q7 Read the two newspaper articles reproduced overleaf, which appeared in *The Times* on consecutive days. Can you think of any reasons why the tone of the two articles is so different? ◆

World's birth on camera

*Despite setbacks in commissioning the Hubble space telescope launched two months ago, **Henry Gee** looks at the promise it holds for reconstructing the first days of the Universe*

High hopes rest on a British centre of efforts to reconstruct the first days of the Universe. The instrument is the Faint Object Camera (FOC), aboard the $2 billion (£1.17 billion) Hubble space telescope, launched from the space shuttle in April.

The FOC detects individual photons of light, recording the position of each one and reconstructing the image digitally. It will be able to probe extremely faint galaxies thousands of millions of light years away.

Light from these sources started its journey when the universe was relatively young, so scientists hope it will reveal what the universe was like in early times.

FOC images from the most distant galaxies could help answer the most perplexing cosmological question of the moment: how matter in a smooth, featureless universe a few million years after the Big Bang coalesced into distinct "blobs" that became stars and galaxies. No object is too faint or distant for scrutiny by the FOC.

"We need only ten photons to say something is there," says Dr Peter Jakobsen, FOC project leader at the Space Telescope Science Institute in Baltimore, Maryland.

The instrument, described by Dr Jakobsen as "an English heritage", is the brainchild of Professor Alec Boksenberg, director of the Royal Greenwich Observatory.

Professor Boksenberg's digital imaging technology first found a place in ground-based observatories, but in the early 1970s he began working with the European Space Agency on a detector specifically for the space telescope.

The result is a powerful instrument that is versatile enough to "cover the whole range of astronomy", Professor Boksenberg says.

Apart from straining to see the most remote galaxies, Dr Jakobsen promises "a tremendous programme" for the FOC. One topic of interest is the structure of quasars, mysterious objects that pack the energy of all the stars in a galaxy into a region little bigger than that of our solar system. This energy may come from black holes buried in the centres of the quasars.

The FOC will be sensitive enough to see whether quasars are the bright, active, central regions of otherwise faint galaxies. The instrument can deploy a special "occulting finger" which blots out the central, bright quasar so that the surrounding material can be seen. The instrument can also double as an ultraviolet (UV) camera and spectrograph which will enable researchers to work out the temperature and chemistry of distant stars and planets in a region of the spectrum that, because of the ultraviolet-absorbent ozone layer, cannot be monitored from the ground.

The spectrograph works in two dimensions to build up temperature and chemistry "maps" of galaxies in unprecedented detail.

Dr Jakobsen finds the UV aspect the most exciting part of the FOC. He looks forward to studying the synthesis of elements in the early universe as well as the chemistry of planetary atmospheres in the Earth's solar system.

However, what will most excite public interest will be the search for planets around stars other than the Earth's sun. There is already a wealth of circumstantial evidence that these planets exist, but no direct confirmation. Unlike the work to be done on quasars and distant galaxies, the planetary search is one of fulfilling expectations rather than breaking new ground.

Professor Boksenberg gives an emphatic "yes" to the question of whether the space telescope will have confirmed the existence of extra solar planets by the end of its useful life, in about 15 years.

Apart from the European FOC, the telescope has an array of detectors that "spans all the tools of the astronomer", Dr Jakobsen says. A high-speed photometer can measure changes in brightness as brief as 20 millionths of a second, and there are two spectrographs, one devoted to UV light. At the heart of the system is the wide-field planetary camera. This has already demonstrated its formidable power by taking pictures of stars of far finer quality than is possible from the ground. The FOC complements the wide-field camera by taking immensely detailed pictures of small areas with a definition equivalent to a focal ratio of up to f288

Even the space telescope's guidance system has been pressed into scientific service. When the telescope singles out an object for study, a set of three fine-guidance sensors lock on to nearby stars to keep the field of view perfectly steady. The sensors are capable of detecting tiny variations in the movement of the guide stars – the sort of motion that betrays unseen stellar companions, such as planets, which have a gravitational influence on the parent star.

Variation such as this has already been detected using ground-based telescopes. For example, the periodic wobble of a faint nearby star called Barnard's Star, six light years away, is thought to be evidence of a very large planet orbiting the star.

The space telescope's accurate sensors should be able to detect much smaller variations, perhaps small enough to reveal the presence of Earth-sized planets.

Given the enormous potential of the project, Dr Jakobsen is relieved that everything seems to be working as it should. "It is fantastic," he says. "There were so many things that could have gone wrong."

(The Times, 28 June 1990)

Nasa to investigate telescope failure

From PETER STOTHARD, US EDITOR, IN WASHINGTON

AN OFFICIAL enquiry is to begin this week into the failure of the mirrors on the Hubble space telescope, a fault which for several years will leave the world's most expensive astronomical device crippled.

The $2 billion (£1.14 billion) Hubble, which is scheduled to cost at least $8 billion to run over its decade-long lifetime in space, was designed to see light from close to the beginning of time. But, as Nasa officials admitted on Tuesday, its light gathering mirror system, said to be the "most precise ever built", contained an error which will prevent it performing better than ground-based telescopes.

An independent review has been launched into this serious embarrassment to Nasa. Even if, as scientists claim, the fault can be rectified by calibrating a new camera to fit a wrongly shaped mirror, the incident will be a blow to an organisation which is always under political pressure to spend less and produce more.

The new camera will not be able to be taken to the Hubble in the space shuttle until 1993, officials predicted. The manufacturers of the mirrors, the Hughes Danbury subsidiary of General Motors, said it was not yet prepared to accept responsibility. "An enquiry is under way," a spokesman said.

"Nobody knows what went wrong."

The fault could be in the main mirror, the secondary mirror, or in the way that the two worked together, the spokesman said. To have tested the mirrors on the ground before launch would have cost more than $100 million and was ruled out because of tight budgets.

The Hubble was launched in April to claims from Nasa that it would revolutionise understanding of the universe, registering light that had been travelling through space for 15 billion years – the time close to the "big bang" with which, according to currently prevailing theories, the universe began.

(*The Times*, 29 June 1990)

Q8 Imagine you are the editorial writer for a tabloid newspaper that thinks that too much money is spent on non-productive science. In 300 words, use the Hubble story to make your views on this issue known. ◆

Francisco Diego is an instrumental astronomer working in the Optical Science Laboratory (OSL) in the Department of Physics and Astronomy at University College London. The OSL has a reputation for making high-precision instruments for some of the world's largest telescopes, including the Anglo-Australian Telescope and the new Gemini Project, which will locate one 8 m telescope in Hawaii in the Northern Hemisphere and one in Chile to cover the southern skies. Diego is currently chief designer for the Gemini High Resolution Optical Spectrograph. His previous achievements include the Ultra-High Resolution Facility (UHRF) for the Anglo-Australian Telescope, the first astronomical spectrometer to measure the wavelength of visible light to one part in a million. In his spare time, he has obtained some of the most spectacular pictures of solar eclipses ever seen.

Francisco Diego

Interview with Francisco Diego

It seems that almost weekly we are confronted with new astronomical discoveries of the oldest galaxy, the largest star, the biggest explosion ever witnessed. To what extent are these discoveries the result of astronomers having good ideas for what to study next as against them simply being down to better and better telescopes and instruments?

I think the relation between astronomical ideas and the equipment available is a two-way interaction. Better instruments lead to better data, but then you can see more and you can see which problems might be interesting and solvable. Looked at historically, astronomy is clearly an observational science. You can't do experiments on the objects you're looking at, all you can do is collect the light they give off and try and understand what you see.

And astronomy has been technology driven. Ancient civilizations looking at the skies might have noticed events and that some of them were regular. But the breakthrough in technology comes when you build, say, Stonehenge with the stones aligned for Sun and Moon observations. Because then you can really see the regularities and, what is more, you can begin to make predictions.

You can see what a huge breakthrough the telescope was because it enabled Galileo to look at Venus and see its phases, to look at Jupiter and see its moons and even the rings of Saturn. Then he knew that the system of Copernicus wasn't just there to simplify astronomical prediction, but that it really corresponded to reality and this provoked a philosophical revolution.

In the last century you had the huge 72-inch telescope built by Lord Rosse, which we are currently repairing after years of not being used. This telescope was the first one to show the structure of a galaxy outside of our own Milky Way and started to give a hint to how big the Universe really was.

Since then we have had the use of photographic plates and even more sensitive detectors.

And since the last world war, the real breakthroughs have come through the use of different regions of the electromagnetic spectrum. Before the Second World War we only used visible light. But after the war, there was first the development of radio astronomy and then – using both satellites and ground-based telescopes – X-rays, the ultraviolet, the infrared and the microwave. That has given us such exciting discoveries as quasars and pulsars and many others.

So when you come to design a new instrument, do you have an overall concept of what you want to do? Are you driven by the new science that you'll make possible?

In practice, we start with the scientific case that has been proposed and we set out then to see if we can design an instrument that can achieve that science. If you take a spectrograph, that is an instrument that disperses light and is one of the main techniques astronomers use because it provides a detailed spectrum of the object you are looking at. In that way you can identify the atoms and molecules that make up the star or gas cloud or whatever it is you are studying. It is a technique first applied to astronomy in the last century when Frauenhofer looked at lines in the Sun's spectrum.

When you are designing an instrument you have to consider a series of trade-offs. The first is what colour range do you want to look at. That is to say, how much of the overall spectrum do you want to be able to study at one go. Against that you have to consider how precisely you want to define the colour – what is the smallest spectral element you want to be able to resolve. And against that you have to consider how faint do you want to go – what is the faintest object in the sky you want to be able to detect. Because if you increase the spectral resolution – the colour definition –

you cut down on the range of colours you can study at one go and you may also make the instrument less sensitive to the faintest objects.

When we designed the Ultra High Resolution Facility, for instance, we particularly wanted a very high colour definition, a spectral resolution of one part in a million. That has enabled us to home in on particular lines in the spectrum very accurately so that, in a giant gas cloud for example, we can distinguish between parts of the cloud moving relative to one another at only a few hundred metres a second, which is slow in astronomical terms. From the exact wavelength and shapes of the lines we measure we can work out the temperature and pressure in the clouds and abundances of the materials that make it up.

Your work has been very successful and you seem to have made things work well almost every time. It is not always like that, though. Take the Hubble Space Telescope. It is now doing spectacular science. But when it was first launched NASA was accused of wasting billions of dollars because the main mirror was found to be at fault. Just how does something like this happen on such a prestige project?

NASA's testing of Hubble's optics was almost foolproof. They took the main mirror and they tested it and found that it focused perfectly. They took the secondary mirror and that also worked fine. The problem was that the main mirror was focusing perfectly to the wrong point for the overall optics design. This had come about because the instrument used to check the focusing of the main mirror had a slight fault in it. And the error was never detected before the launch of Hubble because NASA did not test the telescope as a whole.

They claim that this was not possible because it would have cost millions of dollars that they just did not have available to spend. Well, you could say that – given the overall size of the budget – that not testing the whole telescope was somewhat negligent. But, as an instrument builder myself, I would also say they had more than their share of bad luck. When there is a fault, but it is not an obvious one, then sometimes you just cannot prevent this sort of bad luck.

Where do you think astronomical instrumentation will go next? What projects will the next generation of instrument builders be working on?

One of the main scientific driving forces, in my view, will be the detection of planets around other stars. By this I do not mean simply detecting planets by seeing their effect pulling and pushing the stars they revolve around, but detecting them directly, in their own right. That means we will probably be looking at more of the same sorts of telescopes and instruments, but much bigger. Today we are building 8 m telescopes like Gemini and 10 m telescopes like the Keck. In the future I think we will be looking at 25 m telescopes.

And in order to get the necessary spatial resolution, we will then be looking to join up optical telescopes in arrays. That is already being done using radio telescopes, where they are now linked worldwide to give very high spatial resolution. But to detect planets around other stars directly we need to be able to see things less than one ten-thousandth of an arc second on the sky. [An arc second is 1/3600 degrees. For comparison, the diameter of the Moon as seen from Earth is half a degree.]

I think seeing other solar systems in this way will have an enormous impact. Can you imagine the psychological effect of being able to point to a small dot, light years away from us, and being able to say 'There is another planetary system'. We are talking about discovering other worlds outside of our own solar system. We are talking about the possibility of other life.

Q9 Francisco Diego seems to feel that astronomy is technology driven as a science. From the point of view of the taxpaying public, why might this be 'a good thing'? ◆

Q10 (a) Explain what is meant by the terms: (i) 'refraction of light', (ii) 'refractive index of a material'.

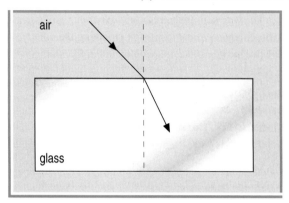

(b) Figure 5.13 shows a ray of light passing from air into glass.

Use the figure to make measurements so that you can calculate: (i) the refractive index of glass, using the ratio sin i / sin r, (ii) the speed of light in glass (take the speed of light in a vacuum to be 3.0×10^8 m s^{-1}).

(c) As the light passes from air to glass, what happens to: (i) the wavelength of the light, (ii) the frequency of the light?

Figure 5.13
Light passing from air to glass

(d) Explain the degree to which the light in Figure 5.13 can be reversed, i.e. travel from glass to air. ◆

Q11 (a) Why do stars appear to twinkle?

(b) An amateur astronomer noted a twinkling of the star Sirius while she tried to photograph it through a telescope. She realized that there were several changes she could make to her equipment or technique in order to try to reduce the twinkling. Explain the expected effect of each of the following changes: (i) using a larger aperture telescope, (ii) using greater magnification, (iii) taking a longer exposure photograph, (iv) taking a shorter exposure photograph, (v) taking the telescope to the top of a mountain, (vi) waiting for Sirius to climb higher in the sky.

(c) (i) The Hubble Space Telescope manager claims the telescope can avoid all the negative effects caused by Earth's atmosphere – is this correct? (ii) State one other advantage that the Hubble Space Telescope offers optical astronomers. (iii) Outline two disadvantages of using the Hubble Space Telescope for observations. ◆

Q12 (a) Explain, perhaps with the aid of a diagram if it helps, what is meant by the terms: (i) 'phase', (ii) 'diffraction'.

(b) Describe how you would demonstrate the effect of passing light through two narrow slits in order to calculate the wavelength of the light. Suggest a suitable practical set-up and include typical values for any measurements you could make.

(c) Observing stars from Earth is a science, but astronomers are not able to control any variables; they are simply passive observers. Explain how observing light from a star can tell us anything about the physics of a distant star. ◆

Achievements

After working through this section you should be able to:

- describe refraction and define the refractive index of a material
- do calculations relating the speed of waves to refractive index
- determine the refractive index of a material
- appreciate the problems associated with chromatic aberration and how telescope design can offer a solution
- describe total internal reflection and know the conditions when it is likely to occur
- outline the main differences between refracting and reflecting telescopes
- describe how diffraction limits the resolving power of a telescope
- describe how two telescopes may be used as an interferometer to improve resolution
- know that CCD cameras enable images to be captured from very low light levels by the storage of photoelectrons
- appreciate that any observation of space is an observation that looks back in time
- know something of the limitations of ground-based telescopes and how technology has opened new observing windows across the electromagnetic spectrum.

Glossary

Achromatic lens A compound lens made with two different glasses to cut down chromatic aberration.

Aperture The diameter of the objective lens or primary mirror of a telescope.

CCD (Charge Coupled Device) A device that allows the energy of single photons to liberate an electron from a pixel and so enable a stored image to be built up electrically.

Chromatic aberration An undesirable flaw in an optical system that occurs when light of different wavelengths is refracted to different degrees, resulting in blue and red light being focused at different positions along an optical axis.

Constructive interference When light rays from two sources meet and combine to produce a more energetic wave of increased amplitude.

Critical angle The angle of incidence at which a ray of light will just become totally reflected within a dense medium.

Destructive interference When light from two sources meet and combine to produce a less energetic wave with reduced amplitude.

Diffraction The spreading out of a wave after passing through a gap or past an obstacle.

Focal length The distance from the centre of a lens to the focal point.

Focal point The place where parallel rays of light are brought to a focus by a lens.

Interference pattern A pattern of places with maximum and minimum displacement caused by the constructive and destructive interference of waves.

Interferometer A telescope comprising two separate dishes whose images are combined to improve resolving power.

Light second The distance that light travels in one second.

Light year The distance that light travels in one year.

Objective lens The light gathering lens at the end of a refracting telescope.

P-type silicon Silicon is a semiconducting material. P-type silicon is made by adding a small quantity of impurity atoms into the silicon structure. This increases silicon's sensitivity to energy. A single light photon will be able to liberate an electron within a slice of p-type silicon.

Phase   This is a reference to the cyclic nature of a wave. Two waves are in phase if they show the same displacement at the same time. They are synchronized. Two waves are 180° out of phase if they are mirror images of each other, one reaching its positive peak at the same time as the other reaches its negative trough.

Pixel   The small unit of space on a display screen or the collecting plate of a CCD.

Prime focus   The location of the focal point for light rays from an object at infinite distance. Rays of light parallel to the lens axis will be focused at the prime focus.

Real image   An optical image produced when light lands on a surface of a detector.

Refraction   When light changes speed owing to its passage through a different medium.

Refractive index   A number representing the ratio of the speed of light through a vacuum to the speed of light through a material. Each transparent material has its own refractive index.

Resolving power   The ability of an optical instrument to distinguish two separate objects. To resolve is to be able to see separate images. Resolving power is often quoted as an angle, meaning the smallest angular separation possible with such an instrument.

Snel's law   This states the relationship of the change in direction of a refracted beam of light to the refractive indices of the two mediums through which the light travels. If the refractive indices are n_1 and n_2 and the angles of incidence and refraction are i and r then according to Snel's law $n_1 \sin i = n_2 \sin r$.

Total internal reflection   When light passing from a more dense medium to a less dense medium arrives at the interface at an angle greater than the critical angle it is all reflected back within the more dense medium.

Answers to Ready to Study test

R1

A red T-shirt reflects red light. On a normal bright day white light falls on to the T-shirt and all colours other than red are absorbed by the pigment in the T-shirt dye. Only red light is reflected and this is what we see.

R2

If only blue light is available to illuminate the shirt this will be absorbed by the pigment in the T-shirt dye. No light will be reflected and so the T-shirt will appear black.

R3

They are both members of the electromagnetic spectrum. They both travel at the same speed, 3.0×10^8 m s^{-1}. Other properties that they have in common include reflection, refraction, diffraction and polarization.

R4

Light from you is reflected off the smooth glass surface. Light from objects behind the window passes out through the window into your eyes. Glass will both reflect and transmit light.

R5

A transverse wave is one that travels in a direction at right angles to the plane in which the medium or field transmitting the wave is vibrating, as in Figure 5.14.

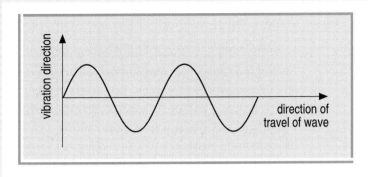

Figure 5.14 Answer to R5

Answers to questions in the text

R6

(a)

Frequency, $f = \dfrac{v}{\lambda}$

$$= \dfrac{3.0 \times 10^8 \, \text{ms}^{-1}}{1500 \, \text{m}}$$

$$= 2.0 \times 10^5 \, \text{Hz}$$

(b)

Wavelength, $\lambda = \dfrac{v}{f}$

$$= \dfrac{3.0 \times 10^8 \, \text{ms}^{-1}}{95.8 \times 10^6 \, \text{Hz}}$$

$$= 3.1 \, \text{m}$$

(to two significant figures)

R7

See Figure 5.15.

Q1

Using

$$n = \dfrac{c_{\text{vac}}}{c_{\text{medium}}}$$

we get

$$1.33 = \dfrac{3.0 \times 10^8 \, \text{ms}^{-1}}{c_{\text{water}}}$$

so

$$c_{\text{water}} = \dfrac{3.0 \times 10^8 \, \text{ms}^{-1}}{1.33}$$

$$= 2.3 \times 10^8 \, \text{ms}^{-1}$$

(to two significant figures)

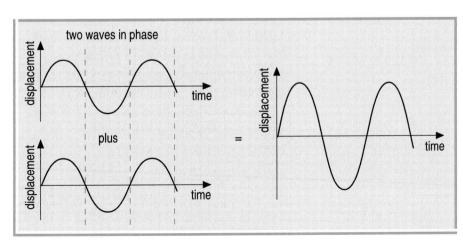

Figure 5.15
Answer to R7

Q2

Light would travel more slowly through flint glass.

Q3

$$\sin c = \frac{1}{1.55}$$
$$= 0.6452$$

therefore

$$c = 40.18°$$
$$= 40.2° \text{ (to three significant figures)}$$

Q4

Surface area is proportional to the diameter squared. So the larger diameter mirror would capture sixteen times as much light.

Q5

$$\text{Resolution} = \frac{\lambda}{d}$$
$$= \frac{0.21\,\text{m}}{10\,000\,000\,\text{m}}$$
$$= 2.1 \times 10^{-8} \text{ radians}$$

This is better than a small telescope, say 100 mm aperture, using white light

$$\text{resolution} = \frac{\lambda}{d}$$
$$= \frac{5.0 \times 10^{-7}\,\text{m}}{0.10\,\text{m}}$$
$$= 5.0 \times 10^{-6} \text{ radians}$$

Q6

$$\text{Minimum aperture} = \frac{\lambda}{\text{resolution angle}}$$
$$= \frac{5.0 \times 10^{-7}\,\text{m}}{2.0 \times 10^{-5}\,\text{radians}}$$
$$= 2.5\,\text{cm}$$

Q7

The first article ('World's birth on camera') appeared on the *Times*'s science pages, so it focuses on the science and emphasizes what the telescope will be able to do despite early drawbacks. It points out the enormous achievements made so far and refers to the 'failure' mentioned by the other article as 'initial teething troubles'.

The second article ('NASA to investigate telescope failure') appeared in the paper's main pages and focuses on the general news aspect of the failure of the telescope to deliver what was promised and on the huge cost of the instrument.

Q8

You could mention the following:

- the cost of the project and how those funds could be spent on humanitarian projects (e.g. the problem of homelessness)
- what use the information gained will be to an average person on Earth (i.e. your readers)
- the telescope is faulty and is costing even more to correct
- it will require maintenance during its 10 year life, so it is a continuous drain on finances
- at the end of its life it will add to the amount of junk cluttering up space.

Q9

Astronomy costs quite a lot of money but it does not seem to provide any practical benefits to the taxpayer who pays for it, if we just look at the science it produces. But if it is technology driven, then we can see if some of that technology can be useful for other purposes besides astronomy.

One example of this is that detectors developed for telescopes are being used in medical imaging. Image enhancing computer programs developed by astronomers are also being used by doctors to give them a clearer picture of their patients.

Much of the equipment that goes up into space pushes electronic techniques to the limit, leading to better components for use on Earth. Mechanical strains on launching rockets are enormous, and the engineering techniques used to withstand them find applications in aircraft and car safety design features.

Q10

(a) (i) Refraction of light occurs when light passes from one medium to another. The speed will change and this can cause the light to change direction.

(ii) This is the ratio of the speed of light in a vacuum to the speed of light through a material.

(b) (i) The value you obtained will depend on how accurately you were able to measure the angles in the figure. This is what we obtained

$$n = \frac{\sin 46°}{\sin 27°}$$
$$= 1.6$$

(ii) The speed of light in glass is less than the speed of light in a vacuum by a proportion equal to the refractive index of glass, i.e.

$$\text{speed of light in glass} = \frac{3.0 \times 10^8 \, \text{ms}^{-1}}{1.6}$$

(c) (i) The wavelength decreases.

(ii) The frequency remains constant.

(d) The path of light can be reversed and it will follow the same path. However, this is only true if the light goes from glass to air at less than the critical angle.

Q11

(a) Stars appear to twinkle because their light is passing through the atmosphere. Different refractive layers of air in the atmosphere cause the starlight to refract by different amounts. We see the result as light appearing to flicker or twinkle.

(b) (i) This would cut down diffraction and give a brighter image but would not influence a twinkle.

(ii) This would simply magnify the twinkle effect.

(iii) This would cause a more blurred image.

(iv) This would give a fainter image, but it would probably be sharper.

(v) This is likely to cut down the twinkle effect as the telescope will be above the dense atmosphere.

(vi) This will cut down the twinkle effect as the light from Sirius will not need to pass through such a thick layer of atmosphere.

(c) (i) Yes it does avoid the negative effects caused by Earth's atmosphere.

(ii) It can see images for 24 hours per day.

(iii) If anything goes wrong it is remote and expensive to repair, and it relies on radio links for remote control and for sending back images.

Q12

(a) (i) The degree to which two waves or signals move together. Phase difference is measured in degrees, so 'in phase' can mean the phase difference is 0° or any multiple of 360°. '180° out of phase' means that the two waves or signals are mirror images of each other – one reaches its positive peak at the same time as the other reaches its negative trough.

(ii) The spreading out of a wave when it passes an obstacle.

(b) I would set up the two narrow slits at one end of a room and project laser light through them. On a distant screen I would measure the distance from the centre of the interference pattern to the position of the first bright fringe, d. I would also measure the slit to screen distance and call it D. Then

$$\text{wavelength} = \text{slit separation} \times \frac{d}{D}$$

Typically the slit separation might be 0.5 mm, the distance to a screen, D, might be 5.0 m and the distance to the first fringe about 5.0 cm.

(c) You might measure the following to find out information about the star:

- the spectral distribution of a star (this would enable you to calculate its temperature)

- the absorption line spectrum (this would indicate the elements present in the chromosphere)

- the Doppler shift in spectral lines (this would tell you the velocity of the star).

If you think back to the beginning of this unit you will realize what a lot of physics you have covered through looking into space. This physics has included grand theories of universal gravitation and the destiny of the Universe, but it has also considered some of the essential ideas of atomic physics, photons, quanta, etc.

Look back at the list of achievements for each section. You should feel able to talk to another student with some confidence about each item listed. If there is an achievement listed about which you are unsure, go back into the section and revisit the ideas. Some of the challenges are not at all easy. The concepts of wave–particle duality, of exponential decay and of spectra were quite possibly new to you. They do make you think twice and reflect on your own understanding.

When you are confident that you have grasped the ideas listed in the achievements sections, ask your teacher or tutor for the exit test for this unit. When you have done the test, consult your teacher, who has the answers and will probably wish to go over some of them with you.

Remember that the physics you have covered is universal; it applies not only to space but to every corner of the physical world. But remember also that physics is a human science. It relies on observers and interpreters, and as understanding grows so does physics. Today's explanations are not the same as those used last century and new ideas in the future will probably challenge those you hold now. The quantum revolution and the expanding Universe, for example, are simply models that have current intellectual value, and like all models they may be improved or replaced. So be prepared to embrace new ideas. The dynamic nature of our understanding of physics is one of its greatest features.

It is around 10^9 years since the birth of the Universe, but people have been formulating science for no more than a few thousand years, and today's physics is only a few hundred years old. We are just at the start of a great intellectual journey.

CONCLUSION

Further reading and resources

Birr Castle: web site address http://itdsrvell.ul.ie/Information/Birr/bshc.html
If you are interested in historical aspects of astronomy, you can find out about the world's largest telescope until 1918, which was located at Birr Castle in Ireland.

COAST: web site address http://www.mrao.cam.ac.uk/telescopes/coast/index.html
For information about the Cambridge Optical Aperture Synthesis Telescope.

Kirchhoff, G. (1859) *Berlin Acad. Bericht*, p. 662. Translated by Roscoe, H. (1870) *Spectrum Analysis*, p. 217, London.

Marschall, L. (1994) *The Supernova Story* (2nd edn). Princeton University Press, Princeton, NJ.

NASA: web site address http://www.nasa.gov/
From here you can access a great deal of further information and images on planets, comets, supernovae, stars.

Acknowledgements

Grateful acknowledgement is made to the following sources for permission to reproduce material in this unit:

Photographs and figures

p. 17: A solar flare – US Department of Navy, Naval Research Laboratory; p. 28: Supernovae 1987A before and after exploding – © 1987 Anglo Australian Observatory; p. 29: Peter Meikle – Peter Meikle; p. 33: Subrahmanyan Chandrasekhar – Science and Society Picture Library; p. 47: Newton splitting white light into its various colours – Mary Evans Picture Library, London; p. 50: Orion constellation showing Betelgeuse and Rigel – NASA/Anglo Australian Telescope Board; p. 54: Jocelyn Bell Burnell – Open University Press Office; p. 62: Louis de Broglie – French Embassy; p. 67: Niels Bohr – Courtesy of Nobel Foundation; Ann Ronan at Image Select; p. 71: Absorption spectrum showing red shift – Royal Astronomical Society, Burlington House; p. 74: Photograph from CoBE showing variations in temperature of cosmic background radiation – NASA Goddard Space Flight Center, Maryland; p. 77: Carlos Frenk – Carlos Frenk; p. 108: Jupiter's moons – Science Photo Library; p. 113: Gaspra – Dr Michael J. S. Belton, National Space Science Data Center; p. 113: Ida – NASA/Science Photo Library; p. 118: Carolyn Shoemaker – Frank Zullo; Science Photo Library; p. 137: Herschel's telescope – Science Museum; p. 137: A modern refractor – Roger Ressmeyer, Starlight; Science Photo Library; p. 139: A 300 mm reflecting telescope – Robin Scagell, Galaxy Picture Library; p. 139: An 80 mm refractor – Robin Scagell, Galaxy Picture Library; p. 144: Merlin array – Mullard Radio Astronomy Observatory, Cavendish Laboratory/Photo: Edward Leigh; p. 144: Interferometer image of Capella – Royal Astronomical Society, Burlington House; p. 151: Francisco Diego – Francisco Diego via Steve Miller.

Newspaper articles

p. 30: 'Supernova cooks the elements', *The Times*, London, 2 June 1987 – © 1987 Times Newspapers Ltd; pp. 52–3: 'More about pulsating stars', *The Times*, London, 11 April 1968 – © 1968 Nature-Times News Sevice; p. 75: 'We find the secret of creation', *Sun*, 24 April 1992 – © 1992 The Sun; pp. 76–7: 'How the universe began', *Independent*, 24 April 1992 – © 1992 *Independent*; p. 115: 'Crash course for Jupiter', *Daily Telegraph*, 29 June 1994 – © 1994 Telegraph Group Ltd, London; pp.116–17: 'Serial killers from heaven', *Guardian*, 7 July 1994 – © 1994 The Guardian; p. 150: 'World's birth on camera', *The Times*, London, 28 June 1990 – © 1990 Nature-Times News Sevice; p. 151: 'Nasa to investigate telescope failure', *The Times*, London, 29 June 1990 – © 1990 Times Newspapers Ltd.

The authors and Management Group would also like to thank Mike Burton and David Tawney for their helpful comments and advice whilst writing this unit.

Index

kinetic energy 15, 19
  photoelectrons 60
krypton 14, 19

Large Magellanic Cloud 29
lead 23
lenses
  achromatic 134–6, 155
  chromatic aberration 134, 136, 155
  focal length 134, 155
  focal point 139, 155
  objective 134, 155
  prime focus 136, 156
light
  see also waves
  blue shift 70
  critical angle 138
  diffraction 82, 139–43, 155
  dispersion 47, 82
  infrared 48
  interference patterns 145–6
  red shift 70, 83
  refraction 47, 83, 131–8
  spectra 47, 63–9
  spectral lines 63–9
  ultraviolet 48
light curve, supernova 34, 36
light seconds 147, 155
light years 147, 155
lithium 14

mass defect 15, 16–17, 19, 20, 36
mass number 16, 22, 37
Meikle, Peter, supernova 31–2
microwave background radiation 73, 83
Milky Way 29
mirrors, focal point 139
models 37
  Bohr atom 67–8
  scientific 12
modulation
  amplitude 54, 82
  frequency 54, 82
momentum 95, 96
  angular 56, 82, 97, 122, 129
  orbits 129

Moon
  centripetal acceleration 102–3
  gravitational field 92
motion, circular 98–101

neon 17
neutrinos 16, 20, 29, 37
neutron stars 51, 52, 55, 56, 83
neutrons 12, 14, 19, 20, 22
Newton, Sir Isaac 47
Newton's second law 100
nickel 32
noise, thermal 147
nuclear energy 14–15
nuclear fission 9, 14–15, 18–20, 37
nuclear power 19
nuclear reactors
  control rods 20
  coolants 19
  fuel rods 18
nuclear warheads 20
nucleon number 16, 22, 37
nucleons 13, 14, 15, 19, 37
nucleus 11, 13, 14, 22, 37

objective lens 134, 155
orbits
  geostationary 106–7, 122
  Hohmann 112, 113
  Kepler's third law 108
  momentum 129
  polar 104, 122
oxygen 17

phase 143, 156
photoelectric effect 58–61, 83
photoelectrons 58–61, 83, 146
  measurement 60–1
photons 16–17, 146
  photoelectric effect 60
pixels 146, 156
Planck's constant 61
positrons 16, 37
power, nuclear 19
prime focus 156
protactinium 24

proton number 22
protons 12, 14, 22
pulsar 52–7, 83

quantum 58, 83
quantum theory 45, 58–62
    Bohr atom 68
quasars 54, 150

radiation
    alpha 20–1
    background 20, 26, 36
    beta 20–1
    black-body 45, 48–9, 58, 82
    gamma 20–1
    light 21
    microwave background 73, 83
    particles 21
    rays 21
radiation pressure 17, 37
radio telescopes 139
radioactivity
    activity 26, 36
    decay 20–8, 37
    decay rate 43–4
    half-life 36
reactions, chain 19–20
reactors
    carbon dioxide 19
    control rods 20
    fuel rods 18
    liquid sodium 19
    nuclear 18
red giants 37, 51, 83
red shift 70, 83
reflection, internal 137–8
refraction 83, 131–8, 156
    light 47
refractive index 131–6, 156
resolution 145–6
resolving power 145–6, 156
    telescopes 142–3
rockets
    launch 110–13
    take-off 93–4

satellites
    communications 106–7
    forces on 95–7
    friction 93
    geostationary 106–7, 122
    polar orbits 104, 122
Secchi, Angelo, star classification 47
Shoemaker, Carolyn, comets 118–19
Shoemaker–Levy 9 114–19
silicon 17
    p-type 146, 155–6
Snel's law 133, 156
sodium
    liquid, fission reactors 19
    spectral lines 66
solar flares 17
solar system, exploration 109, 113
spatial resolution 83
spectra 82
    absorption 63–6
    emission 63–6
spectral lines 63–9
Spica 49
spin 129
stars
    angular momentum 56
    Betelgeuse 48, 49
    black body 48–9
    Capella 145
    Doppler effect 70–2
    main sequence 17, 36, 51
    neutron 51, 52, 55, 56, 83
    pulsars 52–7, 83
    quasars 54, 150
    red giants 17–18, 37, 51, 83
    spectra 48
    Spica 49
    temperature 16, 17
    white dwarfs 33, 51, 52, 55, 83
strong nuclear force 13, 37
Sun 16–17
    Doppler effect 72
    light spectrum 47, 48
    spectral lines 66
Supernova 1987A 17, 28–34